To Roddy

with best wishes

from

[signature]

March 1998

THE CROCUS KING

E. A. Bowles
of Myddelton House

Bryan Hewitt

Bryan Hewitt

THE CROCUS KING

E.A. Bowles of
Myddelton House

The Rockingham Press

Published in 1997
by
The Rockingham Press
11 Musley Lane,
Ware, Herts
SG12 7EN

British Library Cataloguing-in-Publication Data

A catalogue record for this book
is available from the British Library

Paperback edition: **ISBN 1 873468 47 4**

Clothbound edition: **ISBN 1 873468 56 3**

Printed in Great Britain
by Biddles Limited,
Guildford

For E.A.B.

"The Crocus King"

All patiently does he invoke in us
To do homage to the Crocus.
The plants he does not understand
Thrive not in this or any land.
Treasures that baffle us he dotes on
And grows amongst his "weeds" at Myddelton.

From *Gardening Illustrated*, 24th May 1930

Acknowledgements

It is customary to preface a book with the author's thanks to those who have assisted him, and I do so with a grateful heart for the generosity I have had from so many. There are seven in the top tier of people to thank: my friend Peter Rooke, historian and author, for invaluable help and advice with my manuscript; the Honorable Gilla Sarson, without whose insistence and enthusiasm this book would not have materialised; and Brigadier Andrew Parker Bowles OBE , for the loan of family papers and for his very kind offer to write a foreword to this book. My particular thanks go to those few remaining close friends of E.A. Bowles who gave me delightful insights of the character of the man: Florence Darrington, his maid and later his cook and friend; Squadron Leader R.J. ("Bob") Sills OBE, a "Bowles Boy" and honorary son to E.A.B.; Charlie Smith, also a "Bowles Boy", later chauffeur and friend to E.A.B.; Professor William T. Stearn V.M.H., his friend and RHS colleague, whose detailed and scholarly article *E.A. Bowles 1865-1954: The Man and his Garden* is the acknowledged basis for any other work on the great man. To these four I am grateful for their friendship and longevity.

Special thanks are also due to Judy Adams, Percy Andrews, Len Aylott, Mrs G.E. Barnes, Christine Barker, Malcolm Beasley of the botany library of the Natural History Museum, "Cuddy" Buttress, Carleton Photographic of Cheshunt for expert processing, Pat Cleaver of LVRPA, Mike Cook, Leslie Dale, Graham Dalling, Peter Deering, Adrian Doyle, John Drake, The E.A. Bowles of Myddelton House Society, Hilary Edelsten, the staff of Enfield Central Library, *The Enfield Gazette*, Dr Brent Elliott (librarian and archivist of the RHS), Pat Evans, Peter Fox, Mike Floyd for the protracted loan of photographic equipment, the staff of Forty Hall Museum, Jack Frost, Jenny Goldstein, Gillian Goudge, Jean Hayes, George Herbert, my father (the late George Hewitt) for passing on to me a love of old things, Barbara Jenkins, Grace Kiernan, Charles and Ivy Kingdom, Peggy and Arnold Jones, Sidney Langford, the Lee Valley Regional Park Authority, Ernie Leighton, Ray Lowe (01992 636152) for excellent photographic restoration, Dorothy Mottram, David Newton and Danni Bruce for word-processing my manuscript, Raymond Perrier, the late Mrs Frances Perry VMH, Alan Pettitt, Eva Radford, Jack Edwards (whose local history books and those of Peter Rooke led to this one), Derek Rye MBE for allowing me to quote from his father Joseph Rye's reminiscences, Reg Slater, Chris Sanders, Geoffrey Stebbings Kew Dip Hort, Jean Tuson, Jennifer Vine, Jack Walpole, Ken Wilson and Mrs Valerie Carter, for her advice on the manuscript.

I must thank the Royal Horticultural Society for permission to use E.A. Bowles's photographs and papers in the Lindley Library, the Trustees of the Natural History Museum for permission to use material from the Bowles MSS in the Botany Library, and *Country Life* for permission to use the photograph reproduced on page 45.

Finally I should like to thank my mother Irene Hewitt for permitting me to postpone the decoration of the kitchen and bathroom so that I could write this book.

Contents

Illustrations

Coloured illustrations between pages 64—65

E.A.B. with fork, basket and dog, photographed before the Kaiser's War.

Foreword

I think of my Great Great Uncle Gussie often as I walk around our small Wiltshire garden. I have here a collection of plants he bred, discovered or were named after him. In my greenhouse I have a *Pamianthe peruviana*, the descendant of the plant my uncle was given seventy years ago by Major Albert Pam.

I am also reminded of him inside our house as on the walls are pictures of flowers and birds painted by him, books written by him and RHS medals presented to him.

If, as I suspect, my uncle is looking back from 'across the wide river' he will be amazed to discover that his name is still revered and his works much admired.

The *My Garden* trilogy of books is about to be reprinted for the third time, mainly for the American market. His book on *Crocus and Colchicum*, first published in 1924, was reprinted in 1952 and 1985. His biography was written by Mea Allan in 1973 which, although well researched and written, would have been a deeper work had my family been more cooperative.

The 'Bowles' corner' at Wisley has been successfully replanted. The Bowles' Cup, awarded by the RHS for daffodils, is much competed for. The Grenfell RHS Medal which he designed in 1919 and which he won many times himself is awarded to leading botanical artists. His name, his plants and his views are often referred to in articles and on television and radio gardening programmes. The 'E.A. Bowles of Myddelton House Society' is flourishing.

Bryan Hewitt's book is the 'icing on the cake.' The author's knowledge of my family is certainly greater than mine or anyone else's. By using interviews and having done a lot of research he paints a light but accurate portrait of my uncle.

The publishing disappointments of E.A. Bowles are well described: Sir Frederick Stern's hijacking and then spoiling their joint book on snowdrops;

and the failure of himself and his great friend and protégé, Dr. William Stearn, to get their book on anemones as far as the publisher.   However, at least my uncle's exquisite drawings and paintings of anemones can be seen in the Lindley Library.

In 1920 E.A. Bowles and leading garden-owners formed 'The Garden Society,' an all-male dining club limited to fifty members. It hasn't changed and the Society dines three times each year when plants and knowledge are exchanged. When I was elected, and I suspect the name of Bowles helped, it gave me greater pleasure than being elected to any other club or society. Queen Elizabeth the Queen Mother, a very knowledgeable gardener, is Patron and often attends the dinners. Her Majesty enjoys talking about my uncle, not least because he was a close friend of another great gardener and President of the RHS, her brother David Bowes-Lyon.

This fascinating book should bring pleasure to many as it has captured the personality of my uncle as well as the atmosphere within Myddelton House and in the garden when he lived there.   Those who have not visited Myddelton House should do so: although his unique and beloved rockery where his ashes were scattered that May morning in 1954 is no more, his spirit still seems to be ever-present.

Andrew Parker Bowles
Malmesbury
November 1996   Wiltshire

1

Bowles and Myddelton

The names of Bowles and Myddelton are intertwined in the long history of the New River. Sir Hugh Myddelton, the great engineer of the waterway, was the first Governor of the New River Company and Henry Carrington Bowles Bowles its last Governor. It was another Henry Carrington Bowles who had given the name of Myddelton to his new house on the borders of Enfield and Waltham Cross.

Before 1613 London's water supply depended upon a number of wells, public fountains and of course the Thames, the water being brought from the river in carts or in buckets by water carriers. Inevitably the water was frequently contaminated and the wells and springs were apt to dry up, a situation which led Parliament to seek an alternative supply of fresh water from beyond the City. In 1604 a former soldier, Captain Edmund Colthurst of Bath, suggested a scheme for bringing drinking water into London from springs in Hertfordshire and Middlesex. This resulted in two Acts of Parliament granting the Corporation of London the power to make a "New River for bringing Water to London from Chadwell and Amwell in Hertfordshire", but it was some years before the method of conveying the water could be agreed. Although Colthurst had been granted Letters Patent by King James I, it was to Hugh Myddelton in March 1609 that the City conveyed its powers and obligations under the two Acts — although Colthurst did become overseer for the work. Myddelton, who was a citizen and goldsmith of London, came from Denbigh in Wales, where he was an Alderman and represented the borough in Parliament. Significantly, he was also a member of the Merchant Adventurers, among whom he intended to raise most of the funds for the project.

The plan was to tap the springs at Chadwell near Ware and at Great Amwell and convey the water by means of an artificial river to Finsbury, the nearest piece of high ground overlooking the City from the north. The Round Pond at Finsbury (opposite Sadler's Wells Theatre) is some 80 feet above sea level and thus the water could be fed into the City through wooden pipes and conduits. As the crow flies the distance from Chadwell Spring to the Round Pond is just over 20 miles but, since the New River followed the contour of 100 feet above sea level, its length when finished was 38.8 miles (it was later shortened to avoid many detours). The project was completed in 1613 and on

Michaelmas Day, 29th September, a formal ceremony and pageant were held at the Round Pond, under the patronage of King James and in the presence of the Lord Mayor and Corporation of London.   Before the floodgates were opened to fill the Round Pond, there was the recitation of a metrical speech, which went into some detail about the hindrances created by Hertfordshire and Middlesex landowners:

> *Long have we laboured, long desir'd and pray'd,*
> *For this great work's perfection; and by th' aid*
> *Of Heaven, and good men's wishes, 'tis at length*
> *Happily conquered by cost, art and strength,*
> *And after five years' dear expense in days,*
> *Travail and pains, beside the infinite ways*
> *Of malice, envy, false suggestions,*
> *Able to daunt the spirit of mighty ones*
> *In wealth and courage: this a work so rare,*
> *Only by one man's industry, cost and care,*
> *Is brought to blest effect, so much withstood,*
> *His only aim the Citie's generale good,*
> *And where (before) many just complaints*
> *Enviously seated, caused oft restraints,*
> *Stops and great crosses, to our Master's charge,*
> *And the work's hindrance; favour now at large*
> *Spreads itself open to him, and commends*
> *To admiration, both his pains and ends,*
> *The King's most gracious love.*

The King had taken a personal interest in the New River, since part of it went through the grounds of his palace at Theobalds, and when the cost began to exceed the means of Myddelton and his associates the King agreed to provide half the cost — provided he received half the profits. The New River Company was formed in 1619 as Britain's first joint stock company and Sir Hugh Myddelton, now created a baronet, became its first Governor. The New River was not an immediate financial success and James's son, Charles I, disposed of the royal shares to Myddelton, but in time the Company became a major property owner, particularly in London.

2

A Huguenot Family

The ancestors of the Bowles family were Huguenot refugees from Châtellerault in Poitou, with the family name of Garnault.   In 1684, the year before the Edict of Nantes was revoked by Louis XIV, some 400,000 French Protestants had exiled themselves abroad to escape religious persecution. Among those who chose to settle in England were five brothers: Pierre, Aimé, Samuel, Michael and James Garnault.   In common with the majority of the Huguenots they were wealthy, intelligent and industrious. In France they had made their fortune as craftsmen jewellers and with it purchased a great block of shares in the New River Company, enough to give them a controlling influence in the government of the New River.

In 1724 Michael Garnault purchased an estate with an Elizabethan red-brick house called Bowling Green House at Bulls Cross in north Enfield. By coincidence a loopway of the New River cut through the garden. It is said that the then owner of the estate had the loopway diverted a few yards, creating a curve, to prevent the destruction of a Tudor yew hedge planted — so far as Gussie Bowles could determine — in about 1500.   Gussie was very fond of these trees.   The young boys and Frances Perry used to help him scrub their massive trunks about the end of November; this brought away soot and loose bark, making the boles gleam like rich mahogany in the winter sunlight.   Of this hedge only four trees remain today the largest of which near the bridge has a huge Wisteria enveloping it with beautiful lilac racemes cascading down it every June.   Once Gussie heard two passers-by remark about it:

"What kind of tree is that then?"
"Don't you know? — That's what they call a blueburnum tree!"

When Michael Garnault died in 1746 the property passed to his nephew Aimé, who was Treasurer of the New River Company.   When Aimé died in 1782 leaving only daughters the property passed to his grandson Daniel Garnault (1737-1786) and on his death to his son Daniel Garnault III (1773-1809).   His heir was his sister Anne (1771-1812) who had married Henry Carrington Bowles on 26th February 1799.   To celebrate their marriage she planted a Swamp Cypress (*Taxodium distichum*) near the Bulls Cross bound-ary wall and at the edge of the pond, which was subsequently drained after a young member of the family drowned in it. This massive tree was felled in the great storm of 1987.

Henry Carrington's family came from Swineshead in Lincolnshire. Their Latin motto *Ut tibi sic alteri* translates "As I do to thee, so will I do to others". The family descended from an ancient lineage; the sixteenth-century Heralds' Visitations describe one Alleyne of Swineshead as "lord of Swineshead and of the several manors within the same called Bole Hall".   One Bolle appears in the Domesday Book as occupying lands in Hampshire, possibly originating from Bouille (then spelled Boells) in Normandy.   Whatever the source, *The Records of the Bowles Family* by William Henry Bowles cites the Visitation of Lincolnshire of 1562 in which Richard Bolle of Haugh, gentleman usher to Henry VIII, is described as Richard Bowles: he may have been a relative.

Henry Carrington was a print-seller and publisher by profession.   His father John Bowles, born in 1701, issued at least two works connected with flowers: Batty Langley's *New Principles of Gardening* in 1728 and *The Florist* in about 1760, re-issued as *Bowles's Florist* in 1777.   By 1777 the thirteen-year-old Henry, Gussie's great-great-grandfather, was helping his father in the business. Their map and print warehouse was at No. 69 St. Paul's Churchyard, which was then the publishing centre of London.   Henry was the third of a succession in the family profession and the most prosperous. According to the snobbery of the period, a country gentleman did not indulge in trade, and it is said that when he married Anne Garnault he scratched out his name on some of his prints.   Some say he even tried to wipe away all evidence of his connection with the print business, calling in engraving plates bearing his name and destroying them.

Anne who was the last of the Garnault line died aged 41, in 1812 and her widower Henry began the construction of the new house.   It is said that Mr Bowles did not wish to be called 'Mr Bowles of Bowling Green House' whereas Gussie told William Stearn that he would have loved such a title. And so the new house, built of the then fashionable white bricks from Suffolk, was named Myddelton House. Upon its completion in 1818, the old house a few yards to the south-east was demolished and the area where it had stood is now called 'Bowling Green Lawn'.   The pond was created by the extraction of gravel to build the new house.

On Henry's death in 1830 the property passed to his son Henry who on his death in 1852 passed it on to his sister's son, Henry Carrington Bowles

BOWLES FAMILY TREE
Bold line indicates the Myddelton House connnection

Henry Carrington Bowles = Anne Garnault
1763-1830   1771-1812

Anne Sarah = Edward Treacher   Henry Carrington
1800-1856   1792-1861   1801-1852

Henry Carrington Bowles = Cornelia Kingdom
1830-1918   1824-1911

(assumed surname of Bowles
by Royal Licence in 1852)

| Henry Carrington 1857-58 | Henry Ferryman 1858-1943 | = Florence Broughton 1866-1935 | John Treacher 1860-87 | **Edward Augustus** 1865-1954 | Cornelia Anne Medora 1868-87 |

Wilma Mary Garnault 1890-1928   =   Eustace Parker 1884-1952

(assumed surname of Parker Bowles
by Royal Licence in 1920)

Derek Henry = Ann de Trafford   Algernon (1) = Daphne = (2) Oliver
1915-77   1918-87   Heber   Wilma   Brian
               Percy   Kenyon   Sanderson
                        1917-95   1st Baron
                                  Poole

| Andrew Henry 1939- | Simon Humphey 1941- | Mary Ann 1946- | Richard Eustace 1947- | Zarah | Jane | Algernon |

Treacher on condition that he assumed the Bowles surname and coat of arms, which he did by royal licence on 21st May 1852. He and his wife had five children, the first of whom named Henry Carrington died in infancy in 1858. Their second child, Henry Ferryman, was born in the same year on 19th December. John Treacher was born 30th May 1860, Edward Augustus on 14th May 1865 and Cornelia Anne Medora on 26th June 1868.

"I was born in this house on 14th of May 1865 and it has been my home ever since," wrote Gussie. "As I was the fourth in a succession of sons and my parents had been hoping for a change of sex, I have been told that my father complained that I was 'another great bouncy boy'.

"At first sight it may seem unimportant and trivial to record here the sequence of ailments which occurred during my early years, however, they had such a permanent and powerful effect on limiting my capabilities and moulding my character that they turned the 'bouncing boy' into a delicate child.

"For instance when I was six months old the two surviving elder brothers had a long spell of whooping cough which had little ill effect on the big boys but left the baby liable to sharp attacks of what was then called croup, a form of bronchial catarrh needing prompt attention with very hot baths, linseed and mustard poultices, syrup of squills and even more homely remedies, the chest rubbed with goose grease.

"When I was eight years old a more serious and unfortunately permanent affliction came upon me as the effect of eye trouble. It was considered to have been caused by an infection of 'Opthalmia' which I caught from my uncle who suffered from a similar attack while I was staying with him. In my case it resulted in severe inflammation and ulceration in my right eye which lasted for several weeks spent in darkened rooms with eye shades and a daily cauterization. When well enough to go to London to consult Dr Critchell, the famous oculist of that time, it was found that the iris was damaged and the cornea scarred and the lens rendered opaque so that the sight was permanently impaired.

"This has entailed the loss of power to judge distances so much that I have been prevented from playing such games as tennis, cricket and becoming a good shot with guns and even to playing billiards well enough to waste time on such things.

"Therefore my parents decided that I was not strong enough to follow my

Above: *Myddelton House in 1890.*
Below: *E.A. Bowles with his parents, sister Medora and brother Henry in 1887. The space is where his other brother John should have been but he was in the Army, serving with General Gordon's campaign in Khartoum.*

elder brothers to Harrow Public School but that I should be educated at home and until I was fifteen I shared a governess with my three years younger sister and we studied such now out-of-date books as *The Child's Guide to Knowledge* — a series of very simple questions such as this: 'What is tapioca?' We learnt the answer and stood up with a back board held against our shoulders to give us flat backs.

"During my period of living in dark rooms I mostly played the piano and learnt to play by ear as I can not see printed music. I continued to practise and have music lessons, but never got beyond playing Beethoven's Moonlight Sonata & Chopin and Mendelssohn's easier works.

"For outdoor exercise my sister and I rode daily on our ponies and I spent all the time I could working in a sunny garden plot filled with bulbous plants.

"In 1881 our vicar became my tutor and I acquired a little Latin and Greek and two years later I was strong enough to go to a tutor who prepared young men for the army & university examinations. After two pleasant years there and making many good friends I had learnt enough mathematics, Greek and Latin to pass my matriculation examinations and become an undergraduate of Jesus College Cambridge in October 1884.

"It had been planned that I should study theology."

So wrote Mr Bowles in the six pages of autobiography which sadly he never finished. It is likely his failing eyesight or health prevented its completion. The vicar he refers to was the Revd Edward Wood Kempe, Vicar of Jesus Church, Forty Hill from 1874 to 1918. It was he who urged the sixteen-year old Bowles to become a teacher in the Sunday School, possessing as he did a natural ability to get on well with children; indeed they surrounded him. So encouraged by his usefulness to the Church, he decided to study to become a clergyman for which he undoubtedly had a strong calling. Theology was not the only subject he studied at Cambridge; Hebrew and Early Church History were curriculum subjects as well. This was to prepare him for a curacy at St. Bartholomew's in London. In his spare time he privately studied entomology, for since boyhood he had been fascinated by the life-cycles of moths and butterflies.

It was in the Cambridge Entomological Society, a group run largely by the students themselves, that Bowles met Arthur Robinson, a law student who was to become his lifelong friend. The local insect-rich terrain of Wicken Fen was

E.A.B. on the steps of Myddelton House, equipped for an insect-collecting expedition to Wicken Fen in Cambridgeshire, in c.1884-87.

ideal for their insect hunting expeditions. His special interest was *Nonagrias* and *Leucanias*.   And it was here that his detailed notes on the little known *Nonagria Typhae*, the bullrush moth, were gratefully published in the Entomologist Record. At college and at home he set up breeding cages in order to have perfect specimens as they emerged from their chrysalis.   A fellow member of what Gussie called "the Bug and Tick Club" was the future Prime Minister, Stanley Baldwin.   Gussie's brother Henry had attended Jesus College a few years before, gaining his BA in 1881, was called to the bar in 1883 and awarded his MA in 1884.

John, his other brother, was serving as a lieutenant in the 32nd Regiment (the Duke of Cornwall's Light Infantry) which had been posted to the Sudan to relieve General Charles Gordon.   In 1882 the British Army had occupied Egypt in response to a nationalist uprising which threatened the Suez Canal, and immediately they were faced by further trouble to the south in the Sudan. An Anglo-Egyptian force had been defeated there by a fiercely nationalist army, led by Mohammed Ahmed ibn Seyyid Abdullah, regarded by his followers as a prophet or 'Mahdi'.   Gladstone's government sent Gordon out to negotiate with the Mahdi, but he was besieged in Khartoum where he was murdered when the Mahdi's men captured it.   The relieving British force arrived two days too late on 28th January 1885.   There were many victims of the Egyptian climate among the dispirited army and Lieutenant John Treacher Bowles was among them.   He had contracted tuberculosis — now easily treatable with penicillin but in those days a deadly disease, for which patients were cossetted in a warm room protected from the slightest breath of fresh air. He was nursed by Medora, his younger sister, but died on 1st October 1887. Shortly afterwards Medora fell ill having caught the disease from her brother. She was sent to Cannes to recover, but her condition worsened and she died on 27th December 1887.

E.A.B. (far left of back row) with members of the 4th Enfield Boys' Brigade which he founded in June 1892, on the steps of Myddelton House.

3

The Night School

Bowles returned immediately from Cambridge to console his parents. He relinquished the ambition to become an Anglican priest. He regularly attended services at Jesus Church. He was appointed Lay Reader in 1894 and Vicar's Warden in 1913, posts which he held until his death in 1954. His friend and fellow chorister, Leslie Dale, recalls that he made it a point never to deliver the sermon from the pulpit, but from the altar steps, where he could have better contact with the congregation.

It was some time in 1888 that Bowles started a night school at 88 Turkey Street, otherwise known as Bentley House. The instigator was his father, Henry Carrington Bowles Bowles, who donated the premises. It was then up to Bowles to round up friends and fellow church helpers as teachers and also to furnish the large rooms with chairs, tables, books and writing implements. Soon boys and young men from the toughest areas like "Brace's Alley" and "Swynne's Row" were attending — regularly totalling seventy in the first year — to learn the three R's and drawing. After lessons, space was cleared for games such as darts, bagatelle, draughts and other amusements.

At the rear of Bentley House lived Henry Aylott who worked as coachman to the Bowles family for over sixty years. His son Len recalled the night school: "The school used to run during the winter months from October to March every Tuesday and Thursday evening. At the break-up in March there was a rabbit supper. Huge rabbit pies, apple tarts, plum tarts and sausage rolls, all made in Myddelton House kitchen, were delivered to Bentley House by the dog cart and set out on trestle tables for the evening feast. Large urns of tea made in my mother's kitchens formed the liquid refreshment. After supper there was a prize-giving of books to successful students.

"Mr Bowles would then entertain the boys with songs at the piano such as 'Come under the old umbrella, Come piccaninnies do!' and 'She cost me 7s. 6d; I wish I'd bought a dog'. We boys knew these so well that we all joined in noisily. Then the evenings were concluded with 'God save the King'."

Records show that on 17th June 1892, Gussie founded the 4th Enfield Boys' Brigade Company, which was connected with St James's Church,

Above: *E.A.B. with Sunday School boys in the garden of Myddelton House in about 1890.*

Below: *E.A.B. posing with children in Japanese costume in the garden.*

Above: *Jesus Church, Forty Hill, Enfield.*
Below: *E.A.B. in the stable yard of Myddelton House
with Sunday School and choir boys from Jesus Church
before their seaside excursion in 1909.*

Enfield Highway. He held the rank of captain and had three lieutenants under him. An average of fifty boys attended the monthly meetings between 1892 and 1897, when the company was amalgamated with the 2nd Edmonton Boys' Brigade.

It was in the midst of all this that Bowles decided to develop the garden at Myddelton House, which until then was a largely uninspired collection of trees and spotted laurels. With his father's permission and the encouragement of Canon Henry Ellacombe of Bitton Grange in Gloucestershire, he began to design the garden and started to collect plants. He could not have had a better tutor.   Canon Ellacombe, a descendant of Sir Hugh Myddelton, was a distinguished horticultural writer and also a shareholder in the New River Company, which met regularly at Myddelton House. It was the good Canon who gave Bowles a plant of the twisted hazel, *Corylus avellana* 'Contorta', having himself been a recipient of a plant of it from its original discoverer, Lord Ducie, who found it growing in a hedge near Bristol. This Gussie planted in a corner he set aside for plants which did not grow true to form, christening it 'The Lunatic Asylum'.   Other inmates followed like the hedgehog holly, an upright form of elder, a laburnum with oak-like leaves, the contorted hawthorn, a golden leaved sycamore and other aberrations.

The by-election of 1889 saw Henry Bowles, Gussie^]s brother, become Enfield's Member of Parliament, a position he held until 1906 and again from 1918 to 1922. It was also the year he got married, his bride being Florence Broughton of Tubstall Hall in Shropshire and of Clay Hill Enfield, but she was more popularly known as 'Dolly'. The rock garden, that stretch of garden to the west of the Myddelton estate beneath the New River, was ideal for tender plants and alpines as it faced south towards his brother Henry's newly-acquired estate at Forty Hall. The two estates were linked by an avenue of lime trees at one time attributed to André Le Nôtre and there was a small bridge at the bottom of the rock garden. Gussie irrigated some of the more moisture loving plants in his garden with an intricate waterfall system, fed by an unofficial leak in the loopway of the New River which flowed through the estate. Three lead-lined ponds were fed and also a ditch before draining into Turkey Brook at the bottom of the meadow.

By 1895 he was buying plants regularly from Hale Farm Nurseries, Barr and Sons and also Thomas Ware of Tottenham of which Amos Isaac Perry was a partner. Amos was the grandfather of Gerald Perry who married Gussie's distinguished horticulturist friend and neighbour Frances Perry *née* Everett. It was about this time that Gussie started to specialise in the growing of crocuses, which he confined to two large frames in the kitchen garden. The domestic

Canon Henry N. Ellacombe

staff had orders to save any oil lamp glasses which became cracked, which he would put over his tender crocus blooms to protect them from the frost. By 1897 Canon Ellacombe was so impressed by the width of Gussie's knowledge and his love of accuracy that he advised him to join the Royal Horticultural Society. This was remarkable considering that Gussie had had no formal instruction and was entirely self-taught. He sent a cheque for £26 5s. 6d. for life membership: this was a bargain for the RHS which he served devotedly for the next 57 years.

In 1898 he travelled to Egypt with sister-in-law Dolly and a Cambridge friend, Charles Shackle. This was not his first trip abroad. He had accompanied Henry and Dolly on their honeymoon back in January 1889, first to Paris then Monte Carlo and thence to Thomas Hanbury's magnificent fourteenth-century palace and terraced botanical garden at La Mortola. The garden was the work of Thomas and his brother Daniel, the distinguished botanist (1825-1875). A third brother, Capel Hanbury, lived at The Gables, Forty Hill. After Daniel's death, Thomas continued to develop the garden at La Mortola. His intentions were two-fold: to undertake serious scientific experiments in acclimatisation, and to make a collection of plants that was both useful and instructive. He saw his garden as a site for the acclimatisation of plants from all over the world: the contemporary wisdom was that sub-tropical plants might be persuaded to adapt to the temperature conditions of northern Europe if they were first hardened off in the halfway climate of a Mediterranean garden. The Hanburys were a Quaker family and, like the Bowles family, they had a great sense of civic responsibility, using their wealth for public benefit. They built schools for the children of those who worked for them and who had hitherto received no formal education. This facility Thomas later extended to all the children of the adjoining villages. La Mortola has been described as the finest garden ever made by an Englishman abroad; certainly Gussie never forgot it. Its wonderfully comprehensive collection of exotic plants, including a collection of cacti and succulents (one of Gussie's passions), occupied a hot open bank and it was acclaimed as the best collection on the Riviera.   It was here that Gussie first saw *Iris unquiclaris (I. stylosa)*; he built a collection of them at Myddelton and even had a white one named after him, though it would appear now to be extinct.   He spent much of the holiday painting the flowers and sketching.

E.A.B. at the age of 81 in 1946, leaning on one of the lead ostriches, which came from Gough House and flanked the bridge over the New River in the Myddelton House garden. Note the patches on the knees of his trousers — photograph by Peter Fox.

4

The Garden Takes Shape

Gussie's love of horticulture and history are obvious in the garden at Myddelton, for everything that is stone or brick tells a story. Part of the rose garden is protected by a south-facing wall called 'The Irishman's Shirt'. This gets its name from the Tudor red-brick pillar with its characteristic narrow bricks and fine lines of mortar at one end of the wall. Gussie added the summer house and matching wall to it and christened it the Irishman's Shirt as the pillar always reminded him of the tale of the Irishman who took a button to a charitable lady and asked her if she would just be so kind as to sew a shirt on to it for him. The pillar was a refugee from the estate of Gough Park, home of Richard Gough FRS, FSA, the renowned antiquarian and was now the property of Gussie's father. When it was erected , having been brought to Myddelton in two pieces on a cart, Gussie had a stone ball added to the capping stone. Once in place he was surprised to see that the ball looked as if it could roll off to the left and viewed from the other side to the right! After investigating with a spirit level, he discovered that the diamond shape of the pillar was causing a optical illusion for the capping stone was perfectly level.

Gough Park was the source of three more treasures. One, a lead boar standing 17 inches high, was one of a pair which stood on the gate pillars of Gough Park either side of the beautiful wrought iron gates, which are still there. It was curiously appropriate that the boar should find a home at Myddelton as the Bowles coat of arms featured a boar whose heart is seen pierced by an arrow. Gussie chose the opposite pillar of the Irishman's Shirt to display it. Alas it shared the fate of its mate when many years later it was stolen from the old conservatory in 1993. King Edward VII's old pew from Sandringham, which stood in the summer house, was stolen in 1996.

Two life-size lead ostriches which stood on the roof of Gough House came to flank either side of the New River by the bridge opposite the boundary wall. We know from invoices that they were made in 1724 by Thomas Manning and cost £7. They are however not correctly modelled as they should not have flight feathers: Captain Gough, father of Richard Gough, was a director of the East India Company and must have had them made from sketches which he or his seafaring acquaintances had secured and either the draughtsman or sculptor went wrong over the feathers. For their own safety they are now housed in the old conservatory.

To cope with the developing garden and its rapidly expanding collection of plants, in 1900 Gussie took on an assistant gardener, who was to work at Myddelton for the next sixty years. His name was Sam Howard.

The soil at Myddelton is less than a foot deep for the most part, the rest is gravel deposited in the Ice Age. "My garden is the driest in England," he once wrote, "and the water from the New River is so hard it can scarcely be called a miracle to walk on it!   Some water one hot summer given to the Rhododendrons in a sprit of kindness killed all but one of them." Continuous irrigation and mulches were essential in order to keep the plants going. An area was allocated to the west of the garden for the quarrying of gravel to mend the paths in the garden.

The early part of the twentieth century was a very exciting period, for plant-hunters were sending back newly discovered plants and seeds from all over the globe and, as an RHS Fellow, Gussie was getting first refusal of the material. He was receiving letters of enquiry from fellow gardeners and crocus bulbs from collectors all over the world. In addition he had also been forging friendships with many of the leading and not so leading lights of the gardening world, among them Miss Ellen Willmott, James Backhouse, Peter Barr, Dr W.H. Lowe, H.J. Elwes, Canon Ellacombe, William Robinson, Gertrude Jekyll, Euphemia Jessopp, the Revd H. Harpur-Crewe, William and George Paul, Amos Perry I & II, the Revd William Wilks, Reginald Farrer and Major Lawrence Johnson. Many more were to follow over the years.

It had been a busy year: he had been elected a fellow of the Royal Botanical Society of London and in the following year he was elected a member of the Scientific Committee. By 1924 in addition to being a member of the RHS Council, he was chairman of the Narcissus and Tulip Committee, vice chairman of the Scientific Committee, vice chairman of the Floral Committee, vice chairman of the Wisley Committee, a member of the Library Committee and a member of the Botanical Magazine Committee and a member of the Pritzel Revision Committee. Speaking of his committee work for the RHS many years later, Professor W.T Stearn said "Bowles' opinion was always held in high esteem because of his wisdom and experience.   The regulation of the Royal Horticultural Society is that a person could be on the council only for a limited period of years, but they waived this rule as they didn't want to lose Bowles's experience and his wisdom. So year after year, quite contrary to the rules, he was maintained on the council of the society. It is a good thing for a learned society to have limited periods of office because I know from one that didn't, how much you can suffer and the society can suffer

The rock garden (left) and the cactus bank — two photographs of 1913 from E.A.B.'s scrapbook.

from it, but it is also a good thing to break the rules if it is to the advantage of the society. Life fellows are always a liability particularly in times of inflation to a society, because they receive all the privileges that are costing a great deal, but Bowles gave back, I think, rather more than he took. Later on he became a little bit testy; on one particular occasion he was outvoted, I cannot remember what it was but everyone remembered the remark that he made. Some unwise person said "Well Bowles that was a popular decision" and Bowles said "Yes, and so was the release of Barabbas!"

About this time Gussie decided to develop further the rock garden, which his father wanted. Receipts in the Lindley Library, Westminster, show that he purchased Kentish ragstone in 1907 to furnish the distant stretch of bank. Never designed to be a 'grand' rock garden, it was constructed to offer as large a variety of habitats as possible, both wet and dry, where Aquatics, Primulas, Ramondas, Cytisus, Cyclamen, Geraniums, Epimedium and Veratrum lived happily. There was also the unusual feature of a 'Cactus Bank' where Gussie grew a collection of Opuntias all year round and which were protected in winter with special frames. Adjacent to the Cactus Bank was a small summerhouse and bench.

An unidentified girl (possibly the young Frances Perry) with the Gunnera manicata growing to its original height in the Alpine Meadow in the 1920s.

Another feature of this area is a vast expanse of field sloping towards Forty Hall known as the Alpine Meadow. Every winter and spring parts of it are now dominated by the snowdrops which have hybridized over the years. In addition there are drifts of snowflakes, fritillaries, crocuses and daffodils and wild geraniums but the plant which commands the most attention is the giant rhubarb — *Gunnera manicata* from Brazil. Planted in 1908, its huge leaves originally grew to a height of eight feet but since the filling in of the New River it can at best attain five feet.

Parts of the rose garden were already paved with York stone slabs from old Clerkenwell streets; Gussie decided to enclose them with a handsome pergola. Photographs in Gussie's personal scrapbooks, now in the possession of the Royal Horticultural Society, show the completed pergola in 1907. On to the oaken posts and cross beams, Gussie trained hardy vines, wisteria, the golden-leafed hop *Humulus lupulus* 'Aureus', various clematis and climber roses.

The centre piece of the rose garden is the old Enfield Market Cross — "dismissed" (as Bowles wrote in *My Garden in Spring*) "from the market-place to make way for a King Edward VII Coronation memorial. After a year or two

The old Enfield Market Cross (left) at the centre of the rose garden in 1909 and (right) the Pergola in 1907.

of unhonoured repose in a builders yard it came here for a quiet time among the roses and makes a splendid support and background for that lovely single-flowered *Rosa laevigata* 'Anemone'."

Between the Irishman's Shirt and Bowling Green Lawn are two large beds which Gussie filled with variegated and purple-leafed plants at a time when such plants were considered virused and undesirable. This area he called 'Tom Tiddlers Ground'. The reason may seem obscure now but in olden days in London, children played a game in which one child stood on a spot and tried to stop other children trespassing on his area. If he failed, he became "Tom t'Idler". The original boastful words 'here we are on Tom Tiddlers ground, picking up gold and silver' have since come to mean in yuppie language, that the speaker has not just the ground but the money, property or business others are seeking. It harks back to Gussie's love of childhood.

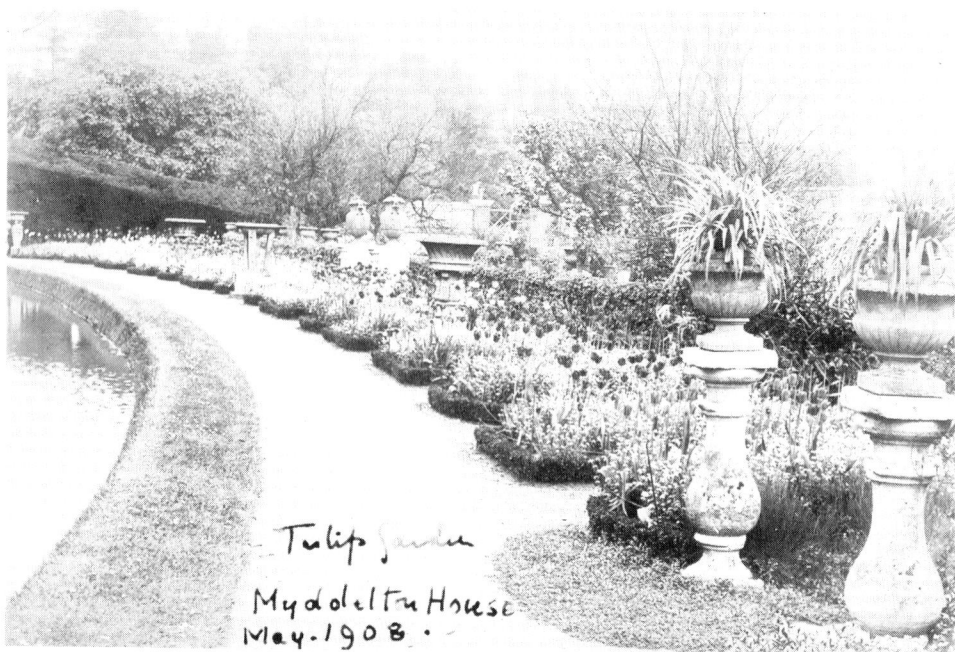

The fifteen box-edged beds of the Tulip Garden following the curve of the New River in May 1908.

Gussie was never keen on Mid-Victorian bedding and the only area he kept formal was the New River Terrace with its fifteen box-edged beds following the curve of the New River and decorated with ornate reconstituted stone planters. The beds were planted in spring with Darwin Tulips and Miss Willmott's deep blue forget-me-nots, and in summer filled with Cherry Pie and geraniums and tall red cardinal flowers. Two beds were always reserved for succulents and some with Penstemon 'Myddelton Gem', a dusky pink with a white throat which was originally described in *The Garden* in 1910. But always in spring these beds played host to a fine collection of tulips, as many as 140 different species and varieties which were always at their best when Gussie opened the garden for the benefit of Forty Hill Church. This was as near as possible to his birthday, 14th May — though sometimes he had to alter the date because the tulips would not oblige by being out on time! This celebrated occasion came to be known as the 'Tulip Tea'. Set in the centre of the wall behind these beds and overlooking what was the kitchen garden and is now the School of Pharmacognosy Garden, are two pieces of ancient stone balustrade which once formed part of the original London Bridge of nursery-rhyme fame. Two rectangular holes cut either side into the stone supported a plank which was a bench in the days of the bridge and the heyday of the garden, whilst above the balustrades Gussie placed the two Grecian lead vases. There is story that one day Alfred Swatton, the head gardener, aimed his blunderbuss at a rabbit in this area and caught one of the vases accidentally in his aim of fire, peppering it with shot. It is still scarred to this day. It is recorded that Gussie was not best pleased by this.

Gussie wrote in *My Garden in Spring* how as a boy "The space between the two great blocks of yew hedge was filled by a steep grass slope very suitable for rolling down when no nurse was on guard, then a wall was built at the foot of the slope and filled in behind with soil and the terrace was formed. It is backed by a low parapet with a wide stone coping on which a row of stone vases stand all the year and a large collection of succulent plants in pots during the summer months."

On the other side of the river, to complement the tulip terrace, Gussie created four large Iris beds, planted with the grey and lavender flowers of *Iris florentina* drifting in to the deep blue purples of *Iris germanica* to the yellows of the intermediate golden fleece leander and yellow dwarf irises. June brought an extension in more varied colours with rich golds replacing the yellow, the mauves, lilacs and pink forms of *Iris pallida* contrasting with white and purple amoenas. The riot of colour made a breath-taking spectacle reflected as it was in the river.

June 1909 saw him plant-hunting in Piora in the Alps with Arthur Bartholomew and Hubert Edelsten, with whom he founded the Enfield Entomological Society at the turn of the century. Calling himself 'Uncle G', he wrote about it in a children's magazine called *Brothers and Sisters*: "As I had never been among Alpine Meadows at that time of year, I soon forgot the rain and cared nothing for how wet my feet were getting; for all the meadows are like the gayest gardens with lovely wild flowers of all the colours imaginable. Yellow and white wild pansies in thousands, great globe flowers wherever the ground is moist, blue harebells three times as large as our wild ones, many kinds of orchids, martagon lilies, purple wild geraniums are everywhere mixed up with ox-eye daisy and clovers red white and pink of many kinds larger and brighter than ours."

It was on this trip that Gussie caught a handsome brown and orange frog which he thought would enhance the lead-lined pools of his rock garden. It was brought home in a tin box, survived and was often to be seen sitting happily on a water lily pad. It was whilst in the Alps that Gussie discovered that the hay fever which plagued him in England cleared up altogether in the fresh Alpine air. To this end Gussie contrived to go plant-hunting in the Alps whenever the pollen count was at its highest, usually accompanied by relatives

The Alpine Meadow bridge across the New River in the 1920s.

or friends and usually in the middle of June. He also had his gardeners pick
the flowers off the Philadelphus. In spite of his one eye, friends were surprised
at his ability to spot a new variety of wild plant faster than most. He would
make sure his newly-discovered treasures were dispatched back to England as
soon as possible with detailed instructions as to their care, so that they arrived
there fresh, ready on his return to be propagated and eventually distributed
among his many gardening friends. He seemed to have an inexhaustible
supply of energy and loved nothing better than clambering over rocks and
marvelling at the treasures he discovered growing in the clefts and thin soils of
hills and mountains. He was not a great plant hunter in the manner of Robert
Fortune or Frank Kingdon-Ward, but such forms of plants as he did return with
are extremely garden-worthy.

The complement of garden staff before 1909 is unclear. Certainly Gussie
was assisted in the garden by the able Sam Howard who started work at
Myddelton in 1900 and retired in 1960. By 1909 it was clear that someone was
needed to co-ordinate the work programme and Alfred Swatton, a Kew man,
was appointed head gardener. Gussie and Swatton were destined never to see
eye to eye but in spite of their differences Swatton remained for forty years,
retiring in 1949.

5

Bowles Boys

It was not only garden matters which were taking up so much of his time, but also Jesus Church where he was member of the choir. Many of the local boys and young men were given the freedom of the garden at Myddelton and were welcome to visit Gussie provided they were either members of the choir, the church or the night school. Not everyone was accepted and the lucky ones came to be known as 'Bowles Boys'. One Bowles boy, Joseph Rye (1896 — 1976) recalled the year 1910 in an essay shortly before he died: "During my later life at school, I had an invitation to go to night school in Turkey street from Mr E.A. Bowles and attended the same for years, enjoying it very much. I think all the boys were very lucky to have Mr Gussie's help at this time. I often wonder how many hundreds of boys passed through the night school and went on to better things. When we were aged thirteen he would take us to St Andrew's Church, Enfield Town, by his own carriage driven by Mr Aylott, for the Confirmation Service. To mark the occasion he would present us with a lovely white tie. After the service we would be taken home by him to tea in the drawing room. The following Sunday we then had to go with him to Jesus Church for the Sacrament. I felt so sorry for the girls who were confirmed as I know of no treat for them.

"When talking about Mr Gussie I always remember how good an entertainer he was, whether he was singing at his piano or reading books to us. Two of my favourites were *Huckleberry Finn* and *Tom Sawyer* by Mark Twain.

"Sunday afternoon outings were eagerly looked forward to when they were spent at Myddelton house. We used to get to the house and, if wet, wait in the Museum-cum-billiard room until Mr Bowles came down. He would proceed to the garden behind the house and feed his pet raven Flo who lived in the uppermost boughs of the trees. Flo would fly down and take pieces of chicken and rabbit from Mr Bowles's hands. On these visits I got to know quite well Kim and Taffy, two Welsh terriers to which Mr Bowles was very attached. We would walk through the garden and over the river down by the rockery and finally through the gate in to the fields and wood. During these walks we were supplied with Clarnico's Caramels by Mr Bowles. He seemed to have an endless supply of these, producing box after box. I am pleased to say all the boys behaved themselves, the older boys helping keep the younger ones doing only what they were allowed with Mr Bowles.

"At other times when we were unable to proceed on our walk he used to take some of us into the house and show us into his study to show us his paintings, birds eggs and butterfly collection and his many books.

"When we went on outings to Brighton, Mr Bowles spent a lot of money on us all. Wherever we went he would foot the bill. In those days we went from the Old Forty Hill Station (now called Turkey Street) and got a special train reserved for us to go right through to our destination. We used to go swimming and Mr Bowles would come in with us. Any who could not swim had water-wings and he would teach us to swim. At Brighton the usual place for tea was at 'Bollo and Bank' and the staff did us fine. They thought as much of Mr Bowles as we did."

Another feature of life at Myddelton was the Cricket Club. Sometime in 1880 a party of boys from the Forty Hill area, members of the Bible Class fostered by Gussie, met Sir Henry in London and were entertained to tea and cakes. Afterwards they were taken to Benetfink's, the sports outfitters, and told to select such equipment as was necessary to set a cricket club in motion. The Myddelton Cricket Club is still flourishing to this day. In 1959 eighty years after its inception Emrys Wilson, son of one of the club's founders, recalled its early days: "In the year 1901 under the captaincy of my father Jim Wilson it was recorded that the team had lost all their matches that season and were duly rewarded with a wooden spoon draped in the traditional red and black Myddelton House colours, presented by Miss Frances Wilson, sister of the captain. This hung in the old pavilion until its demolition four or five years ago."

The Aylott family had four brothers playing at one time, Henry, Walter, Ben and Len. In Arthur Luff there was batting talent that would grace any cricket ground. "Harry Gudgeon (captain for many years), Bob Moran, a clever slow bowler, Harry Clay, Jim Large (the baker) played well without a break throughout the whole of the season. Len Aylott in his day was a very formidable wicket keeper and his "Ow-zat?" must have been audible to the landlord pulling up the pints at the 'Pied Bull'. The wicket was never roped off so the cows would meet on the newly-mown pitch and discuss how much milk they each would supply towards the players' teas. A large shovel was always at hand before the start of any game and the farm yard pump and whitewash bucket were useful to any fielder who had the misfortune to be up-ended in a difficult attempt at catching or stopping he ball. Also worthy of note were Jack Walpole a fast right arm bowler, Ted James a fast left arm bowler and big hitters Charlie Curtis and Silbert Howard."

*The only known photograph of E.A.B. with the Myddelton Cricket Club —
pictured here in 1932 — from the Len Aylott collection.*

A fixtures card for the Myddelton Cricket Club season in 1889 lists Capt.
H.F. Bowles, MP as president.   By 1903 Gussie was president of the
Myddelton House Juniors CC whilst the fixtures cards for the 1930s reveal him
to be president of the MHCC. He did not in fact show any interest in the games
nor the football club (now defunct) which also ran at this time, though he does
make a surprise appearance in the middle of the cricket team photograph for
1932.

The cricket AGMs were in two parts, recalled Peter Deering: "There was
an unofficial AGM which was held in the Plough public house in Turkey Street
and at that meeting all the business of elections etc. would take place & then
a week or so later by official arrangement the official AGM would be held in
the library in Myddelton House and Gussie was the president so he took the
chair. And of course the whole thing was a farce in a way because the secretary
would go through the agenda in a formal manner and proposals would be made,
votes taken and I recall Gussie saying ' this must be the finest cricket club in

the country: we never have any dissenters it is so well organized!' I think we did it that way out of respect for him. We didn't want to bore him or argue in his house and say things about other people in front of him, he was a great churchman after all, which is why only away games were permitted on Sundays and without the Myddelton title — so it would be for instance 'Sixer Slade's Eleven'."

In 1910, Gussie founded the Forty Hill Mutual Improvement Horticultural Society. The object of the society was to "promote and encourage the advancement of horticulture in general and the rearing of domestic livestock". Monthly meetings were to be held with discussions, lectures and exhibitions; membership was by proposal and election and subscriptions were one shilling per year. The first show was in August 1911 of cut flowers, plants, vegetables, live stock and the best home-made loaf. It was held at Myddelton House Gardens in the cowshed. One can visualise the preparations the night before, clearing and cleaning out the dirt floor of the cowshed to make it a fit venue for the show. Outside a long table was placed to accommodate the long line of children's jam jars filled with wild flowers. The children were encouraged to capture queen wasps and white butterflies for a reward of one penny each. The total amount of prize money was £4. 2s. 0d.

Meetings were held originally in the night school (88 Turkey Street), and more often than not Gussie would be giving the talk. Margaret Deering remembered "a few men stood around an old iron stove, an oil lamp suspended from the ceiling gave only enough light to see one another and a long trestle table was in the middle of the bare room with forms alongside the table. Mr Gussie arrived and with him came Mr and Mrs Washington who lived in the cottage nearby. Mr Gussie made us welcome and we all sat down to listen to his talk on bulbs of all sorts. He had specimens which were handed around (some did not manage to get the whole way round we noticed ...)"

Gussie was president for 44 years until his death in 1954 and Frances Perry succeeded him, both holding the highest award the RHS can bestow — The Victoria Medal of Honour. The society is still thriving and currently has a member of the Bowles family, Charles Kingdom, as its president.

Gussie's generosity to the people of Forty Hill and Bulls Cross and especially the poor is legendary: his parents had instilled in him their maxim that there should be 'no privilege without responsibility'. They had been devoutly Christian and Henry Carrington Bowles Bowles had sat on several charitable committees from the 1850s onwards. Gussie followed suit

A presentation to William Radford in appreciation of his many years as secretary of the Forty Hill Mutual Improvement Horticultural Society—from left: E.A.B., Mr Harris (head gardener at Forty Hall), George Banks, Mr Radford, Herbert Way (the Society's new secretary), Mr Cooper (gardener at Capel Manor) and Mr Land.

involving himself in several local and national charities.   In addition he inherited and ran a scheme started by his father called 'The Coal Club'. Quite simply he would buy coal at the pithead cheaply, have it brought to Forty Hill Station and one ton delivered to those members who paid sixpence a week. Sam Howard collected the subscriptions and the participants would have enough coal to see them through the winter. Florence Darrington, who started work at Myddelton in 1925 as Gussie's kitchen maid and later cook, staying twenty years, recalled another kindly act Gussie did annually: "Braces Alley was the biggest slum you ever saw, people wouldn't go there: it was not dangerous but poor.   Mr Augustus used to go down there bringing joints of beef and blankets to the needy there at Christmas. Some of those people used to come up and used to sit along those forms down in the basement and beg for help. Sometimes they would only get a shilling. Up on our floor, the bedroom floor at the top of the house, there was a chest and I often used to sit up there when I went up to change in the afternoons. There were all these letters written by a lot of those people written on wallpaper just torn off! Mr Bowles used to supply them with ordinary cloth, Oxford shirting, so that they could make clothes and sometimes he gave them boots. I don't think he ever looked upon himself as anything different from anybody else. He was very down to earth. And he couldn't tolerate people who tried to put you down. He was a man of the people. He was always a gentleman."

The Bowles family always vacated Myddelton House in September when the servants took it turns to have their holidays. "I am driven out!" he would write to his friends when announcing a visit. August 1911 saw him visiting the Munstead Wood home of Gertrude Jekyll and Gravetye Manor to stay with William Robinson, the editor of *The Garden*. Much of the Myddelton garden is greatly influenced by Robinson's pioneering naturalistic approach, deploring as he did "how far we have diverged from nature's ways of displaying the beauty of vegetation".

Gussie's mother Cornelia died in October 1911 at the age of 87 — he had kept vigil by her bedside till the end. She had been a large and jolly woman, a collector of fans and postcards and was passionately fond of cooking, preferring to use not the kitchen but the morning room, where she happily experimented with new recipes surrounded by pots, pans and an open fire. She also made milk dishes for the poor and sent bunches of grapes and nectarines from the hothouses to the sick. So large did Mrs Bowles become that when standing she could not see her feet. She had frequent falls and when concerned friends rushed to her assistance she would remark cheerfully "you see my dear, it doesn't matter because I bounce!" It was certainly a sadder house for her passing. Perhaps it was then that Gussie resolved to keep Myddelton exactly as she had known it. Gussie had no use for electricity, the telephone or gas light.

With only two exceptions he simply pretended that the 20th century had not happened. Those exceptions were the motor-car and the wireless. Until the 1930s he was still using his horse-drawn brougham but the gift of a Standard car from his sister-in-law, Lady Bowles, caused him to sell his two covered carriages and open landau for £1 each to a local scrap metal man, who went on using them with the Bowles coat of arms for weddings. A wireless run on a accumulator battery arrived in the house during the war and it became routine for Gussie to listen to the one o'clock news before returning to his gardening. Gas was fitted on the departure in 1945 of the cook Florence Darrington. Her replacement was Hermione 'Mina' Wiltcho, an Austrian refugee, who scorned the kitchen range which though it served Myddelton perfectly well demanded blacking, a process which took an hour every morning. Mina was adamant it had to be gas and her cat! As cooks were scarce

*Florence Darrington (left) who worked for Gussie from
1925-1945, first as kitchen maid and then as cook in
succession to Edie Dean (right).*

Gussie was forced to capitulate, but gas *only* for the cooker!   Even so Gussie
berated the gasmen in no uncertain terms for their lack of care in tearing up his
lawn.   Until the end, oil lamps and candles were the order of the day at
Myddelton.   Another thing Gussie preserved was Mr John's room.   Since his
brother's death everything was kept just as he had left it, his uniform hanging
up along with his helmet, sword and guns and Egyptian campaign medals.   In
another room, perpetually locked — 'The Room of Memories' —were all the
dresses of bygone years: Medora's presentation gown, ball gowns, Mrs
Bowles's wedding dress and veil and boxes of exquisite lace.

6

A Question of Attribution

In December 1912, a letter arrived from the editor of *The Gardener's Chronicle*, R. Hooper Pearson, inviting Gussie to write three or possibly four books about his garden.   The result was the celebrated garden trilogy *My Garden in Spring, My Garden in Summer* and *My Garden in Autumn and Winter*.   Gussie's approach in writing the trilogy was original.   He was taking an imaginary visitor round Myddelton on a tour that included every part of the garden, chatting about his plants as friends and regaling the visitor with amusing stories and where this or that one came from or how he had found them tucked away in some crevice of a mountain.

For the preface to *My Garden in Spring* R. Hooper Pearson asked Reginald Farrer to oblige.   Farrer and Gussie had met five years before at an RHS show and had plant-hunted together in the Maritime Alps and Mont Cenis district.   Indeed, Farrer had dedicated *Among the Hills*, the record of their plant-hunting expedition of 1910 to his friend: "Ave Crocorum Omnium Rex Imperator Paterculus Augustus" — "Hail to thee of all crocuses King and Emperor, little Father Augustus".   Thus he neatly acknowledged Gussie as the greatest authority on the genus, 'Little Father' being a version of their nicknames for each other and fellow plant-hunting friends being aunts and uncles.   Although fifteen years older than Farrer, Gussie was Farrer's 'nephew' and Farrer Gussie's 'uncle'.   Farrer's preface lavished praise on Gussie's garden, but it began with a strong attack on a very different sort of creation:

"There are nowadays so many gardeners that gardens are growing every year more rare. Everyone must have their 'rock-work' and the very rich are out to purchase the glories of the Alps at so much a yard — with all the more contentment if the price be heavy, so that their munificence may be the more admired."   Only on the third page of the preface did he come to the garden of his friend, Gussie Bowles.   "The soul of the real garden lies in the perfect prosperity of the plants of which it is the home, instead of being merely ... the expensive and unregarded colour-relief of its titanically-compounded cliffs of stucco and Portland cement.   Come into Mr Bowles's garden and learn what true gardening is, and what is the real beauty of plants, and what the nature of their display ... visit Mr Bowles's garden at almost any moment of the year, and wander past great tuft after tuft of the rarest and most difficult brilliances that

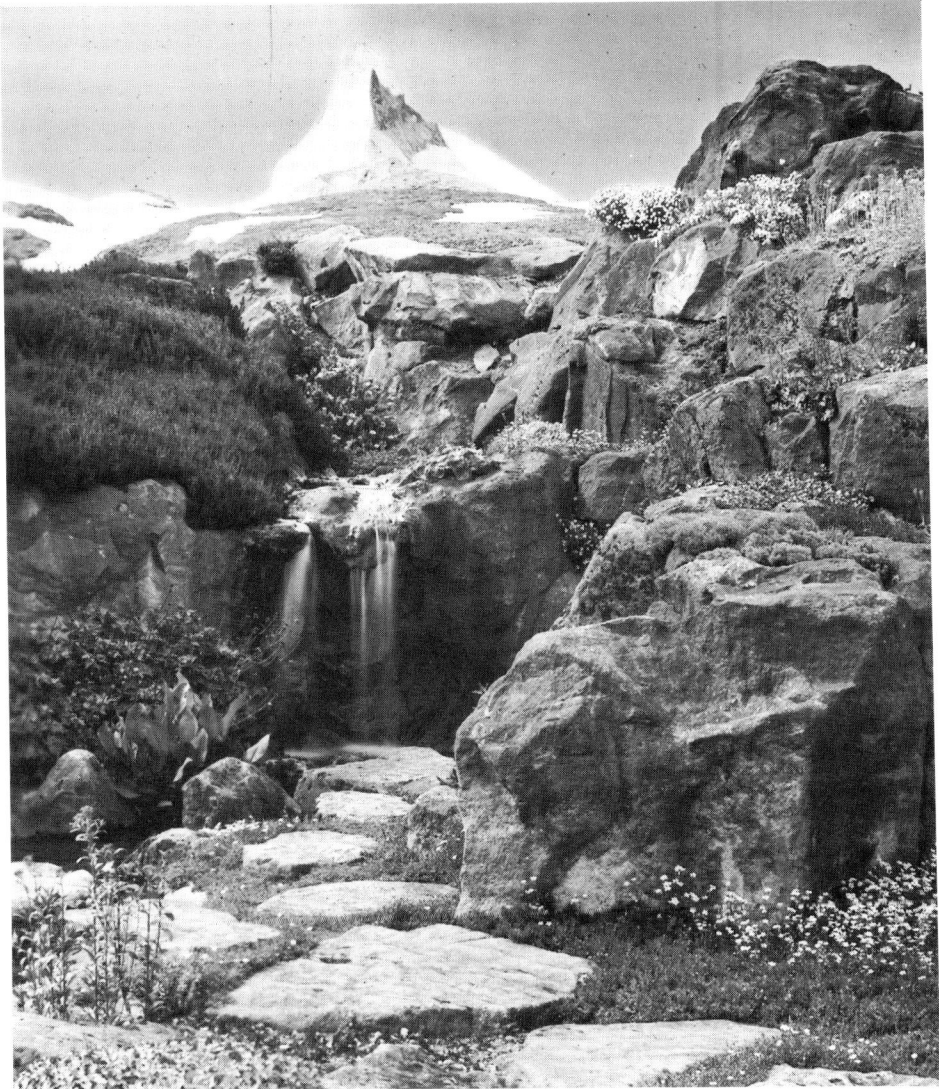

Sir Frank Crisp's "Matterhorn" at Friar Park, Henley-on-Thames (copyright: Country Life Picture Library).

have quite forgotten they are rare or difficult at all or in exile, but are here making individual masses individually beloved and tended as full of rich colour and of love of life as they were on the Cima Tombea or the Col de Tenda"

One man who took offence at Farrer's words was Sir Frank Crisp. Crisp was a renowned Alpinist who had spent a fortune creating a scale model of the Matterhorn, using 7000 tons of millstone grit and Portland cement, complete with a little tin chalet, and to imitate snow the summit was clad in alabaster

Left: Sir Frank Crisp of Friar Park, Henley-on-Thames, and (right) Gussie's friend, Reginald John Farrer.

chippings.   The edifice filled the four-acre estate at Friar Park near Henley. Though Farrer hated it, the plants adored it for one visitor counted 400 species in flower.   A lawyer by profession, Crisp had made many generous contributions of plants to Wisley, he was treasurer of the Linnean Society and until then a friend of Gussie's. *My Garden in Spring* was launched in the spring of 1914 and Crisp rushed into print with an eight-page quarto pamphlet which he and Ellen Willmott distributed at the gates of the second Chelsea Flower Show.   It was a vicious attack on Gussie, headed in large lettering MR E.A. BOWLES AND HIS GARDEN and subtitled "A New Parable of the Pharisee and the Publican".   Crisp clearly held Gussie responsible for the attack on his rock garden when he wrote: "It is fashionable nowadays to give 'Living Pictures' and none could be more interesting than a Tableau of the Temple, illustrating the old parable — the Pharisee in one corner pouring out his fervent thanks that he is 'not as other men are, extortioners, unjust, adulterers, or even as this Publican'; with Mr Bowles in the other corner, equally fervent in rejoicing that he is 'not as other Rock Gardeners are, carpet bedders, 'pavement patterners, gambolers in purple and gold, who care nothing for culture, or rarity, or interest in plants, or even as this poor Publican of Friar Park,' of whom no doubt he is sick of hearing and reading."

Crisp goes on in the pamphlet to publish favourable reports of Friar Park by the Grand Old Man of English gardening, William Robinson and other leading Alpinists and writers, finishing his attack with: "we may add how much discomfort (to say nothing else) might have been saved to Mr Bowles if he had remembered that to show he is a righteous man, it is not necessary to establish that his neighbours are evil-doers". But in a mean footnote on page two is a *non-sequitur* which beggars belief: "there is a reason to believe that the special pique of the extract we have above given from the preface to Mr Bowles's book originated in the fact that we declined an offer from the writer to buy for £250 (!) a plant of *Daphne repestris* and added to our offence by not responding to other invitations that equally did not appeal to us."

The scandal and furore was unprecedented in the world of horticulture. In a letter to Gussie dated 14th May 1914 (Gussie's 49th birthday) Crisp wrote:

"I cannot imagine what evil genius possessed you to make that malevolent attack upon me, when I have never said or done anything otherwise than in praise of yourself and your garden — indeed very much so. I regret you did it because 50 years of controversial strife in my own profession prevents the possibility of my not hitting back again when I am hit first, and the same number of years experience has hardened me to always giving back even more in return — contrary no doubt to the scriptural instruction. Criticism I do not object to and there are points in the criticism which you issued which are well worth consideration, but why you were not content to put it in the ordinary way of criticism, but felt obliged to give it a personal turn, I cannot understand nor can the numerous horticulturists who have written me on the subject and who are equally astonished (to use no stronger term) at your action, though they are ready to make allowance for the probable fact that you allowed yourself to be led away by a stronger will without giving it sufficient consideration. As the matter has formed such a subject of comment in the horticultural world I am sending copies of the enclosed to all the leading horticulturists and Robinson is issuing it in 'Gardening Illustrated'
Yours Truly
Frank Crisp"

Gussie wrote back immediately:

"Dear Sir Frank,
I am exceedingly sorry to learn that anything in the preface to my little book has annoyed you. I must ask you to believe that it is the very last thing I should wish to have happened for you have shown me such constant kindness

ever since I first had the pleasure of meeting you. I hope you will think better of me & dissociate me from any intention of malevolence when I tell you that, as I was not publishing the book myself, only delivering the MS to the publishers and the editor, I thought I could not interfere with the preface written for them — further than request that the personal allusions might be omitted. If you think I could and should have intervened to prevent its publication (as this most unwished for outcome make me now desire I had done) you must please attribute my failure to do so to my ignorance of literacy etiquette.

"When I read the preface I did not notice anything in it I thought went beyond F's usual way of writing, rather lucidly against things he does not like. Now in the light of your letter, I must own I see some of the sentences can be read in a way displeasing to you and I apologise most sincerely to you that I had not the sense and good feeling to see this possible annoyance before."

But Sir Frank was not for turning when he responded on 18th May 1914: "How can an author escape responsibility for a preface to a book immediately following his name as author and immediately preceding his own writing?"

The day before Gussie had received a telegram from the Revd William Wilks (1843—1923), Secretary of the RHS "Your letter received and is all that you could be expected to say after the event whilst accepting it in the spirit in which you have written it. You must not forget that an author is responsible for the preface to his own book. No one would have cared for anything Farrer wrote and I should not have noticed it as he is recognised to be a crank. It was only your endorsement of him that made the stir."

R. Hooper Pearson, editor of *The Gardener's Chronicle*, which published Gussie's response, wrote to him saying "I have made certain suggestions, which would have the effect of making your reply shorter than it reads at present: yet, I think, it would leave your apology as ample as anybody could expect it to be.

"In speaking to quite a number of people about this affair I find that there is a general sympathy for yourself, and surprise that Sir Frank's criticism was not directed specially against the writer of the Preface. I have written to Sir Frank pointing out that I could not see any attack on Friar Park in the Preface until I read it in the light of the circular he sent me, and, of course, I have expressed my sorrow that there was anything in the volume that was calculated to give him annoyance and displeasure. I have hinted that it might be possible in the second edition to reconsider some of the passages."

He added a couple of postscripts:

"The *Summer* volume looks exceedingly attractive.

"The criticism of the *Spring* vol. will have a very good effect on the sales!!!"

The 22nd May brought another letter of staunch support from the Revd Joseph Jacob:

"My dear Boy I am sorry I did not see you at Chelsea — Wilks told me of Crisp's scurrilous and 'below the belt' attack on you, but I did not read it until in the train on the way home. I enclose a copy of the letter I have sent the brute by tonight's post. What a magnificent show it was! The best Chelsea has ever seen. Yours ever Joseph Jacob."

Jacob's letter to Sir Frank Crisp:

"Sir, As a member of the Horticultural Club I write to say that I sincerely hope the report is true that you have resigned the post of President. After your scurrilous attack on my friend Mr Bowles, I think it is the best thing you can do. I am yours Joseph Jacob."

It would appear that Sir Frank's final word on the matter came to Gussie in a letter dated 22nd May:

"The remaining thing now requiring to be done in order to bury your connection with the matter (Farrer I shall of course keep alive) is to have some not private statement as to your disclaimer of the preface. I had printed 5000 copies to be issued with the 'Guide' during the year to visitors coming to Friar Park but I will gladly cancel these if you will give me the opportunity of doing so. What I can do would be to quote only the italicised preface and then say 'Mr Bowles disclaims etc etc'. This however is entirely for you. I am however quite ready to incur the expense of a re-print if it would be more congenial to your views. Yours truly, Frank Crisp."

Gussie made a note at the foot of this letter to record the content of the next and probably his last on the affair:

"I feel further circulation could not annoy or injure me. But I should value the cancelling of your proposal as a token of your acceptation of my explanation and your forgiveness for any annoyance I unwittingly caused you."

The previous day, Gussie had written an explanation and apology to Sir Frank for publication in the 13th June edition of *Gardening Illustrated*. He ended the letter by saying:

"I think it only fair to myself to point out that the wording of Sir Frank's protest makes it appear to anyone unfamiliar with the book and the preface, that I had myself made an attack upon him and that I had wanted him to buy a plant off me at an exorbitant price. Whereas, as a matter of fact, I have made no attack on him whatever, and I have never offered to sell him (or anyone else) a plant at a high or low price, for I have never sold a plant yet and I hope I never shall." He finished by offering Sir Frank "my sincerest apology as far as anyone can apologise for the words of another".

William Robinson, the magazine's editor, wrote to Gussie on 27th May:
"Like others of your friends, I regret this incident very much: no one I hope will suppose that it was you who offered the daphne for 250 pounds? The story was about before your book came out and you are not a nurseryman. The best way is to let the thing 'die out'. It has arisen wholly from Farrer's too facile rush of words often without clear aim." Whether the two men resolved the matter amicably is not known.

What is obscure in all this is Ellen Willmott's support of Sir Frank against Gussie. We may read between the lines of her earlier correspondence in the mid 1900s that she was perhaps "setting her cap" at Gussie, for in undated letters to Gussie she wrote:
"My dear Mr Bowles, a line in great haste, come when it suits you best Mr Pae was so delighted when I told him I would invite and tell you he was coming here with a view of combining your visits. Could not you arrange to stay a night here and look at books and talk?"

And in another letter: "I wish I could persuade you to come to me for Sunday the 8th and do some gardening. We might have such a Happy Daff day. I have so much to say to you on kindred subjects also. Sat & Sun evening we could talk and look at the pictures of Croci, etc."

Ellen was certainly a handsome lady, a talented gardener and passionate rosarian. As she was author of the celebrated monograph *The Genus Rosa* and only seven years older than Gussie, they seemed entirely suited. Indeed Farrer had told him "really you'd better marry the cankered Ellen at once and save further trouble". For whatever reasons Gussie did not heed his friend's advice. Perhaps his life was filled sufficiently with all his committee work, the garden he was apt to spend all day in weeding, his parochial duties, writing, painting and the local lads who would visit him every weekend. Had he married his diverse energies, varied interests and talents probably would not have developed and Gussie himself would not perhaps have found personal fulfilment. It is far more likely that Ellen's alliance with Sir Frank Crisp was because she felt they had been jointly insulted by Farrer's preface. Her rock garden at Warley had been designed by Richard Potter of the Backhouse Nursery, who had

Miss Ellen Willmott of Warley Place

designed part of Crisp's rock garden. Her rock garden was also characterised by massed planting. A further link between Crisp and Willmott was William Robinson, who accepted Crisp's diatribe for publication in *Garden Illustrated* and described the rock garden at Friar Park as "the best natural stone rock garden I have ever seen." Robinson was the most public advocate of the principle Farrer was most concerned to attack: the massing of colour in the rock garden. As a parting shot to the affair — referring to a carnation that bore her name — Gussie wrote rather mischievously: "'Ellen Willmott' requries disbudding and fussing over beyond our practice."

My Garden in Summer followed later in 1914 and the final volume *My Garden in Autumn and Winter* was published in 1915. Frances King, author of *The Well-Considered Garden*, summed up the trilogy well when she wrote "it is impossible not to be caught up by so strong a wave of enthusiasm for plants and the growing of them as sweeps along these pages. The writer's learning and his delight in his gardening pursuits are everywhere in evidence; yet all is so spontaneously told that learning and delight are equally agreeable to the reader. There is in his books a true ecstasy in gardening."

The "Spring" volume sold well, though doing little financially for Gussie who in his innocence sold the copyright for £80.10s, receiving similar sums for each of the two subsequent volumes. The £87.10s for *My Garden in Summer* he donated to the Jesus Church Seating Fund to replace the existing pews with oak benches. Later in life when Gussie wanted to re-issue the trilogy with comments on what plants had died and so on, the publishers or their successors said they did not wish to re-publish, and would only do so if he would buy back the copyright. As he could not afford to do so, the world has been deprived of one of the masterpieces of horticultural literature.

7

The Kaiser's War

It must have been a great relief when on 8th June, 1914 he left Dover with his friends the Garnett-Botfields to go plant-hunting in the Alps. It was on this trip that Gussie made a happy discovery. At La Grave the party stopped to look at the church, a lovely little building most picturesquely situated, and the Garnett-Botfields went inside to inspect it. Gussie wandered around the churchyard. The ground was covered with a double flowered creeping buttercup and amongst it was a beautiful periwinkle. Though it was not in flower he was impressed by its broad foliage. The following May at Myddelton it put forth bright blue flowers, so lovely that Amos Perry introduced it as *Vinca minor* 'Bowles variety'. Gussie always joked it was the only occasion anyone could accuse him of grave robbing!

Later the following year Farrer in Northern China sent back seeds coded 'FARRER F,13'. This was *Viburnum fragrans,* the now venerable specimens of which are still in the middle of the Hollow Lawn forming a circle around a large *Ginkgo biloba*. Although long known under the illegitimate name *Viburnum fragrans*, since 1966 it has been correctly called *Viburnum farreri*.

In August of that year war was declared. Gussie always referred to it as the 'Kaiser's War' as opposed to the Second World War which he called 'Hitler's War'. Many of his boys were now fighting 'over there'. He spent much of his time writing to them and sending them such useful items as razors and pens. He was touched by their letters of thanks and an old cabinet at the top of the stairs became filled with albums of them. In his study he had a gallery of their photographs taken in their uniforms, hanging around the mantelpiece and tucked in to the sides of the big mirror. It was an echo of when they were boys and he had made a gallery of their silhouettes with enlargements all around the huge room of the night school.

By 1915, with his father increasingly less able to fulfill his commitments, Gussie was attending meetings of the Cottage Hospital and the Anne Crowe Almshouses and he represented the Middlesex County Council on the governing body of Enfield Grammar School. As well as being Vicar's Warden of Jesus Church, he was now a trustee of Enfield Parochial Charities.

In quieter moments, Gussie could be found in the garden and frequently in the rock garden area sitting with his easel and brushes, painting a watercolour of an iris, crocus or snowdrop; there was so much to capture as the three large boxes of mounted prints now in the possession of the Natural History Museum bear testimony. His paintings portrayed not only the plants but dead birds picked up in the garden and hung by their feet in his lavatory till he painted them.   The staircase at Myddelton was crammed with his watercolours lining the walls like postage stamps — Gussie liked to call them "the early Bowles's."   In his bedroom there were some beautiful paintings of Haarlem he had done on a visit.   Professor Stearn was once contacted by the Dutch government which was interested in acquiring them, because they showed some old buildings beside a canal which the Germans had widened during the Second World War so that the tanks could not cross it.   Gussie's paintings were the last record of the houses which were destroyed in the process.   At this time, he was also producing his watercolours for his articles in *The Garden*, working with the aid of a magnifying glass for the sight in his left eye was now failing.   'Notes from

William Morley, butler to the Bowles family for forty years.   "His unfailing readiness to assist in organising fêtes, cricket matches, flower shows and other events was the mainspring of their success and an assurance of a feeling of welcome to those attending them.."   He died in 1938.

Myddelton House' was the title of his articles.   *The Garden* honoured him by dedicating the 1918 volume to him.   The excellence of Gussie's contribution to the RHS, encompassing detailed research of a wide range of plants, his committee work and watercolours over the previous twenty years was rewarded in 1917 with the highest award of RHS, the Victoria Medal of Honour.

Meanwhile on the Western Front "Bowles Boy" Fred Ponsonby of Goat

Lane received the following letter from Gussie:

"Dear Fred,

"I was very pleased to get your letter with your new address so that I can write to you again.   I have just got back from a little holiday.   I went on Thursday to Edinburgh to stay with Professor Balfour at the Royal Botanic Gardens.   You can guess how I enjoyed seeing those wonderful gardens and all the rare treasures in them & that I did not come away without some of the treasures & promises of more.

"Then on Saturday I went to Mr Farrer's home at Ingleborough in Yorkshire and saw some of the plants he has been raising from the seeds he got in China.   I helped him to plant some of them out in his rock garden.   I brought away a large box full of treasures from there and hope to be busy attending to them tomorrow.   Willie Vanson has been up to see me — as he wants to get back into the Lock.   We had a pleasant afternoon at Radford's Nursery — on 1st September for the Hortl. Soc^s Meeting — such a lovely fine evening & the roses and the apples looked well.   We missed you and Will and Lennie.

"Hopefully next year's meeting you will be with us again.   It was Rose Showday at the RHS today, & I was delighted with some of the newer ones, which looked tip-top in spite of all the bad weather we have had lately.   I wonder whether you will come across good old Bill Radford — I hope you will. It's a pity you can not be together.   The harvest was looking splendid up North & it was mostly cut, and some of it stacked — they have had a long drought in Yorkshire, which helped them to get forward with it.   They had burning hot days in July while we had all the rain.

"Well good luck to you old Fred and be sure and write back for anything you would like me to send you.

"Your Old Friend
E. Augustus Bowles"

Twenty-three days later, on 4th October 1917, Fred Ponsonby was killed in action, aged 19.

The "good old Bill Radford" mentioned in the letter was Eva Radford's older brother.   A pupil of the night school and fellow Sunday School teacher at the church, he was serving with the 7th Battalion, the East Kent Regiment

(The Buffs). His company had stopped at the town of St. Jon Ter Biezen for the evening to rest. It was 23rd September 1917 and Bill had received a food parcel from Gussie and had left the trench to rest and eat. Suddenly a German aircraft dropped six bombs on the camp and of the 89 men in the company, 26 were killed and 63 wounded. Among the wounded was Lance Corporal William Radford, whose arms and hands were maimed and whose jaw had to be reconstructed from a photograph. A padre told him later that if he had not left the trench he would have been one of the fatalities. Bill was three and half years in hospital and later married one of his nurses. Gussie had encouraged him to start his own nursery for which he was saving, but his disability sadly destroyed that possibility.

On the 1st February 1918 Gussie's father died in his sleep following a stroke which had left him partially paralysed; he was 87. The townspeople gathered to watch the funeral, lining the route from Myddelton to St. Andrew's Church, Enfield Town, where he was laid in the family vault in the churchyard. There was a touching simplicity brought to the proceedings for the coffin was laid on an open farm cart pulled by estate workers. At the church the Union Flag on the tower was at half mast. It was the end of an era. Henry Carrington Bowles Bowles had been the last Governor of the New River Company until in 1904 it was taken over by the Metropolitan Water Board. In his will he left £373,486 — the largest donation of £2,000 to Jesus Church to build a new chancel in memory of his wife, £500 each to Enfield Cottage Hospital, the Samaritan Free Hospital and the City of London Hospital for Diseases of the Chest. To his servants who had been with him ten years £100, and £50 each to those who had been with him five years.

The Revd Edward Wood Kempe, Gussie's friend and mentor who took the service, died three months later from a heart attack. It was a sad blow, coupled with departure of the Kempe family, but a sort of legacy came to Myddelton in the form of Alice Mears, one of their maids. Alice was a dedicated housemaid and it is doubtful if Myddelton had ever been so clean. Gussie liked to have vases of grasses — "I used to throw away his grasses, he was cross!" she recalled with relish. He also liked anemones in their fluffy state and one day he came in to find the hall and stairway in a cloud of floating seeds. "Alice has been at it again" became a regular saying at Myddelton.

An annual maintenance task was for the pond to be cleared out, a job not for the gardeners but for Gussie and the boys. For this they wore bathing costumes, Gussie's being of Edwardian vintage with blue and white rings reaching down to his ankles; a straw hat with his college ribbons completed the outfit (it was the same hat in which the boys picked strawberries). Everyone enjoyed ploutering about in the muddy water, pulling up the water lilies and other pond plants which had grown too big. There were so many water lilies in those days (recalled Charlie Smith, one of the last wave of Bowles Boys) that ducks could run across on the lily pads from one side of the pond to the other. Once the task was completed, Gussie would trot across the lawn and indoors through the open bay window of the Morning Room, dripping mud as he went. Charlie remembers once when still dripping, Gussie drew his chair to the fire and put his feet in the hearth. At that moment, Alice came in to mend the fire at her appointed time. "It's all right," her master told her. But Alice was methodical and stood waiting, bucket in hand. Bowles refused to budge, whereupon the exasperated housemaid emptied the coal over his knees and stumped out. After a pause, Gussie remarked: "it looks as if poor old Alice is upset".

In 1920 came the retirement of Frederick ('Toggy') and Nellie Eastaugh as Master and Mistress of Forty Hill School. They had served the school for 42 years, having arrived in Enfield from Suffolk as newly-weds. Gussie was one of the Governors and used to pop in to see how the children were getting on and sometimes would present the top-of-the-class prizes. Gussie was sorry to see them go but kept in touch, frequently being chauffeured to their new home in The Grangeway, Winchmore Hill. An article in one of Gussie's albums, from the *Evening News* dated 9th January 1950, reports the couple celebrating 72 years of marriage; by then 'Toggy' was 95 and Nellie 93.

Perhaps the best known and certainly the favourite of all the Bowles Boys was Robert John Sills, a choirboy who remembers his first visit to Myddelton at Christmas 1919. "I was eight and we stood outside singing carols. The choirmaster was Sid Bentley — 'Old Bent Legs' was his nickname, since an accident had stunted his growth. Consequently his feet could not reach the organ pedals, so he used to get off the bench and dance on them. Indeed so low did he sit in his car that it looked as though his trilby was doing the driving!" Morley admitted them and they sang Gussie's favourite carols, 'God rest Ye Merry Gentlemen' and 'The First Nowell'. Bob lost his mother when he was only two-and-a-half years old and his father died four years later, so from an early stage he was looked after by his great-aunt, Florence Sills who ran The Turkey public house. To Bob, Gussie became 'Uncle G', a name he still affectionately calls him after 70 years. Gussie occasionally took Bob with him to London in the school holidays. First they would be driven to Enfield Town Station — in the brougham if raining, in the landau if fine. At Liverpool Street Station they would board an 11E bus for Fleet Street and Hoare's Bank,

*"Bowles Boy" Bob Sills in the rock garden of Myddelton House with E.A.B.
and his life-long friend, Arthur Robinson.*

where Gussie would draw a month's wages for his staff, attaching the notes to
an inside pocket with safety-pins. Then it was on to Vincent Square where Bob
would be left to amuse himself while Gussie attended a meeting. Afterwards
they would stop off at the Army and Navy Stores for lunch and shopping. It
was the Army and Navy Stores that supplied Gussie with his false teeth until
he was put on to a dentist in Bullsmoor Lane by Charlie Smith. The excursion
would be completed by a visit to some place of interest like the Royal Academy
in Burlington House or the British Museum.

8

Aunts and Crocuses

Gussie, it must be said, had little time for women unless they were keen gardeners, although he would never be rude to the opposite gender. However, four women featured quite largely in his social life. Lady Beatrix Stanley was herself a keen gardener with a special interest in bulbous plants and she was not averse to staying in the cold rooms of Myddelton House in the winter just to see the flowering of a new bulb. Nor did she mind roughing it with Gussie on his plant-hunting trips. He affectionately called her 'Aunt'. Another lady who did not mind roughing it was 'Aunt Susan', Mrs Susan Garnett-Botfield, the intrepid wife of a military gentleman. She was a seasoned traveller, plant collector and Gussie's friend from the 1910s until his death.

Then there was Nellie Sansom, Gussie's half-French cousin, charming and bird-like in appearance and a talented artist who exhibited regularly at the Royal Academy. She it was who painted the portrait of Gussie which was presented to him during a party at Myddelton in December 1924. It had been subscribed for by a large number of parishioners. She was also endearingly kind to the staff at Myddelton and the boys who would frequently be invited to join Gussie and any distinguished visitors for tea. This was always Lapsang Soushong, which the boys did not like much preferring the 'Oatmeal Rounds' Gussie had made for him by Florence Darrington.

And, of course, there was Frances Everett who had come to Myddelton as a shy school girl to beg some leaves for a dried collection she was making. Gussie acquiesced and pointed out the rarer trees to her. A visit to Chelsea Flower Show shortly afterwards decided her that she wanted a career in horticulture. Gussie suggested Swanley Horticulture College. "You'd better start right away as a garden boy," said Gussie, "come and do some weeding". It was the best possible start to be allowed to weed among Gussie's treasures and have regular access to Gussie's library and the accumulated wisdom of his 40 years in horticulture. Frances went on to marry Gerald Perry of the famous Enfield nursery family and became the first woman member of the RHS Council in 1968. Her published works were required reading for several generations of gardeners. She once told me that Gussie had said: "You know, Frances, I look on you as one of my boys!" "I never really knew how to take that," she added.

E.A.B. plant-hunting in the Pyrenees with Major Walter and Mrs. Susan Garnett-Botfield ("Aunt Susan") in June 1927.   Below: E.A.B. with Lady Beatrix Stanley ("Aunt Bea").

From upper Burma in October 1920 came the sad news of Reginald Farrer's death.   Farther from civilization than ever and alone except for his native servants, he had stayed on to complete his seed harvest and explore the frontier ranges between Burma and China.   The weather deteriorated and because of the mist and the rain visibility was down to a few yards.   He had travelled over a thousand miles and collected 400 plants specimens and under such conditions his strength failed him. He fell ill at Nyitadi, possibly from bronchial pneumonia, and his most loyal servant, Jange Bhaju, ran without stopping for just under four days to fetch medical supplies but arrived back only a short while before

Farrer died on the 17th October. His servants carried his body down and laid him to rest in Konglu above the old fortress. For Gussie it was a tragic end for a man who was probably his closest friend. He was only 40.

*   *   *   *   *

The origin of the word *crocus* is believed to derive from a mixture of ancient names for the Iridaceous flower. It is supposed to be the *karkom* of the *Song of Solomon*, which is *kurkuma* in Sanskrit. *Crocum* is the form used by Clusius, while the Greeks chose *krokos*. The Saffron Crocus (*Crocus sativus*), which this name designated, is of great antiquity and obscure Mediterranean or Near East origin, going back to the Bronze Age. *Saffron*, the word used for the stigmata from the crocus, comes from the Arabic *za'feran*.

Saffron was greatly valued in ancient times, as now, for use as a medicine, perfume and flavouring, and as a brilliant yellow dye. It was said that one grain of good Saffron contains the stigmata of nine flowers, so that one ounce would represent the produce of 4320 flowers. During the Middle Ages severe laws were enacted against the adulteration of Saffron: the Saffron inspectors of Nuremberg caused one Jobst Findeker to be burnt in the same fire as his adulterated Saffron in 1444, while in 1456 two men and a woman were buried alive for a similar offence.

For centuries, Saffron was grown commercially at Saffron Walden in Essex. Miller's *Gardener's Dictionary* of 1768 states that the price of Saffron was then thirty shillings a pound, and that the net profit from an acre of Saffron crocus was about £5 4s. a year, without counting any return for the sale of surplus roots. By 1790, however, the Saffron trade at Saffron Walden had completely ceased. At about the same time the cultivation of vines for wine making also died out. Professor Stearn suggests that this may have been due in part to foreign competition, both Saffron and wine being more cheaply produced in southern Europe; but he suggests that climatic changes might also have contributed to the decline, for the Saffron crocus in Victorian gardens did not flower so frequently. A major Saffron growing area today is northern Greece although the British climate, becoming warmer again, now allows it to be grown commercially in Wales.

No serious study of the genus *Crocus* had been undertaken until an important paper by A.H. Haworth on the cultivation of the crocus appeared in the *Transactions of the Horticultural Society of London* in 1809. Understanding the genus as a whole has largely resulted from the work of Haworth (1786-

1833), Joseph Sabine (1770-1837), Jacques Etienne Gay (1786-1864), William
Herbert (1778-1846), John Gilbert Baker (1834-1920), George Maw (1832-
1912) and E.A. Bowles.

In the short time between 1901 and 1920, cultivation and advancement of
Crocus forms had moved apace. Gussie's collection for the year 1895
numbered 135 named species and varieties. By 1909 he had almost all the
known Crocus species that could be grown in the British Isles, in addition to
the endless hybrids of his own raising. He raised a whole series of *Crocus
chrysanthus* and *biflorus* seedlings which he named after birds: Bullfinch,
Golden Pheasant, Siskin, White Egret, Yellow Hammer, Kitiwake, Snow
Bunting, Blue Throat, Black-Backed Gull and Golden Plover. In addition he
raised Opale, Blue Rock, Moonlight, Khaki, Shot and Bumble Bee. In 1923,
he received the Veitch Memorial Gold Medal for his work on Crocuses,
Colchicums and other plants: but perhaps more importantly to him it was also
the year he found two pure white *Crocus sieberi* seedlings growing in the rock
garden where he had not sown any seed, after thirty years of careful experimen-
tation in his crocus frames without success. "That," he once said, "is just
Nature's way of telling you 'I can do these things better than you if I choose,
though you imagine you know all about the *scientific part*'."

It was about this time that the publishers Martin Hopkinson & Co. were
inviting authorities on various genus to produce handbooks on their pet
subjects. William Dykes wrote *the Handbook of Iris* and Gussie's *A
Handbook of Crocus and Colchicum for Gardeners* followed in 1924 (price
12s. 6d.), with a second edition in 1952. It had eleven coloured plates of his
own watercolours and seventeen in monochrome. Though much more
detailed than the *Garden* trilogy and accurate in every detail it was not a
taxonomist's book, but essentially a guide for gardeners to the peculiarities, the
horticultural merits, the garden forms, how you could cultivate them and keys
to help you identify them once you had put them into the right group. And
because people were always confusing Crocuses with Colchicums, he added
a section on Colchicums. Gussie would always point the difference (not
without irritation) saying "the Colchicum belongs to the Lily family and shows
it by having six stamens, while the Crocus, an Irid, has only three, and if people
don't know the difference I won't give them a thing."

In a talk on Crocuses given to the RHS on 11th February 1936 he said:
"I should like to say something about what some of my friends call 'Crocus
Fever'. Some charge me with giving it to them, but I assure you that I do not.
I give them crocuses and I leave the fever to develop. It is not a dangerous

disease, although if you get it badly, it lasts throughout the year. It is not a germ I can carry about to infect you with; it is simply the charm of the Crocus itself. So be warned, and if you do not want to have Crocus Fever do not look at Crocuses."

The Bowles Boys were encouraged to take an interest and given the job of lifting and sorting crocus corms for drying. Emrys Wilson remembers they would have to get the earth off them and put them in boxes. If they were special crocuses, marked on the labels with three stars, they would go in specially marked boxes. Gussie had no favourites for this job, which was important to him, but gave the boys a turn each, four at a time. Sometimes he would require only one helper, and one boy would arrive, then another and another. He would say: "One boy's a boy, two boys is half a boy, and three boys is no boy at all!" He would survey the gathering gang: "Well, I expect you'd like to go and get the cricket things".

Many years after Gussie's death, Bob Sills was reading the crocus handbook when he got a pleasant surprise. In the chapter about *Crocus tommasinianus* he read: "One with a white tip to its pale lavender segments looks like a piece of Wedgwood china when examined closely, and bears the name 'Bobbo' to remind me of the sharp-eyed boy who was the first to spot it." Gussie named it after him but had not told him for whatever reason.

In 1925 at the suggestion of his "nephew" Dick Trotter, a fellow crocus enthusiast and RHS committee member, Gussie began a new book, this time on anemones. Soon he was turning out exquisite pencil drawings of them, for which task Bob Sills regularly sharpened the pencils to long points. Then when 'Uncle G' had finished a drawing, Bob was allowed to blow on a fine spray of gum to fix it. Gussie's researches took him to Kifissia in Greece where *Anemone horrensis* grew, his party including Dick Trotter, Lady Beatrix Stanley and Dick's sister Lova. Sadly the book was never completed; possibly the subject was too large for one man to take on.

Meanwhile the garden at Myddelton still played host to scores of Bowles Boys. There was so much to amuse them as Reg Slater recalled: "I was talking to him one day near the New River when along the path came one of the youngsters, rod in hand. Gussie looked at me and smiled and said: 'Broke me 'ook, Sir'. Sure enough, as he came close, the first words he uttered were 'Broke me 'ook, Sir'. Gussie produced a packet of hooks from the pocket of his Norfolk jacket and sent the young fisherman happily on his way. I remember another occasion strolling along the river path with a friend Fred Hyatt behind these youngsters sitting on the bank watching their floats intently.

Boys in bathing costumes on the Pond Lawn where they were helping Gussie remove the excess pond vegetation.

Now Fred was a born mimic and could not resist interfering in some way with the boys' pleasure. Standing on the path was a watering-can. This was too much for Fred, who filled it from the river and imitating Gussie's sing-song voice proceeded to walk behind the fishermen watering their heads arousing them to cry 'Pack it up and clear off.' But Fred persisted, he repeated the process about three times. I thought he was tempting Providence, when he re-filled the can by stooping beside the boy at the end of the row. 'Pack it up,' he said and gave Fred a push. The effect was dramatic — Fred turned a complete somersault, watering-can and all, and with a tremendous splash disappeared in the river. He came up clutching the can, weeds dripping from his ears and scrambled to the side where I pulled him out. Fred had had enough; he squelched off to the house where Gussie gave him a bath and dry clothes. He reappeared dressed in a pair of Gussie's flannel trousers, a Norfolk jacket and a trilby with the brim turned down and proceeded to shamble around giving a hilarious imitation of Gussie who joined in the fun. There were many occasions when we would sit in the study with Gussie in the glow of the oil lamp, and he would ask Fred to do his impressions, and Fred would oblige with various animal noises and caricatures of local people. One of Gussie's favourites was Fred's impression of a vicar who 'had a font put in at the east as well as the west end of his church with the result that we can now baptise babies at both ends'."

Another activity was skating on the New River and the pond. Leslie Dale remembers Gussie teaching Bob and himself how to skate on the New River: "We used metal chairs from the pond terrace to lean on and push along in front of us while we were skating. We didn't need a chair much because we soon got the hang of it all and Gussie was a beautiful skater. He used to do what he called the 'Dutch roll', just rolling along without taking his feet off the ice. On one occasion on one of the lakes in the woods the ice was beginning to thaw, it was bending, and we said to Gussie 'we're not going across there again, it's too dangerous'. He said 'no, I think we can do it once more'. So he went roaring across and when he got to the middle of the lake the ice broke and he went right in it up to his waist almost. He managed to get out by breaking all the ice around him, covered in mud up to his waist and roaring with laughter. We went back to the house and he went in had a bath and cleaned himself up: he thought it was huge fun."

Leslie had met Gussie through the Church of England Men's Society, whose meetings were held in his library once a month. "He used to have a service of what he called preparation for Holy Communion service the next day and there was about a dozen of us, including Emrys Wilson, Harold Wilson, Horace Edwards, Dennis Edwards and a few others. We used to have a lovely little service and Gussie used to give us a short talk, call it a sermon if you like, and he used to play the harmonium while we sang about three hymns."

Back in 1919 Gussie had been invited to design a medal in commemoration of Lord Grenfell, who was standing down as President of the RHS His design was accepted and struck in versions in bronze, silver and silver-gilt. It is awarded for exhibits of pictures or photographs of horticultural or botanical interest. Gussie was a recipient several times: in 1929, 1931 and 1932 he received the Silver Grenfell for paintings of flowers and in 1933 the silver-gilt for furred and feathered inhabitants of the garden. In 1928 an exception was made for his floral paintings and his Grenfell Medal was struck in gold.

In March of that year he holidayed in the South of France where he visited Major Lawrence Johnson's garden at Serre de la Madone, then on to the Hanbury garden at La Mortola. It had been 39 years since he had seen it and he was delighted to find it still the paradise he found it on Henry and Dolly's honeymoon, despite the sad gaps caused by a frost.

There is an article in Gussie's scrapbook entitled 'Impressions of English Gardens in 1928', written by Mrs C.S. Houghton of Massachusetts, U.S.A. for the *Bulletin of the Garden Club of America* published in November 1928. It reads: "Come then to Myddelton House, the garden of Mr E. Augustus Bowles, M.A., F.L.S., F.E.S., V.M.H., the writer of *My Garden*, — familiar

E.A.Bowles's paintings of crocuses (top) and colchicums.

E.A.Bowles's painting of "Anemones miniatures" in 1928.

The great variety of the paintings and drawings of E.A.Bowles.

Above: *The memorial reredos in Jesus Church, Forty Hill, Enfield.*
Below: *Myddelton House today in the ownership of the Lee Valley Regional Park Authority.*

book of four seasons; the possessor of so sure a knowledge of rare bulbs that he not only magically flowers them, but vies with Mr Galsworthy, reproducing them in pastel. Indispensable hard worker in the Royal Horticultural Society, friend alike to amateur gardeners and village boys, he truly epitomizes the spirit of helpfulness which all must feel who journey to Waltham Cross. Perceive in the picture the old house among shade-trees of paternal planting; adjacent the towering holly hedge; the lawn that was once a bowling green; the river, a limey canal bordered with high tulips; the little box-edged rose garden centred by that ancient market cross of Enfield, fittingly preserved by Mr Bowles. Beckoning us to a natural looking rock garden was a huge dazzling *Magnolia stellata.* We beheld there for the first time the wonderful sky blue poppy *Meconopsis baileyi* — that great perennial of the Himalayan mountains, of breath-taking beauty this nineteenth of May. We followed a lime-tree walk to the beautiful vista of a brother's house and park. Returning came a flagged terrace with railing and steps leading down to an informal lily-pond. This railing was graced by very old urns containing most lovely pale blue sprawling *Solanum crispum.* It was a garden of much feeling. Then we were conducted to a Victorian drawing room where, amidst precious old Bow and Chelsea, we delighted in the special tea and lively conversation of Mr Bowles."

Martin Hopkinson, the publisher of the *Crocus Handbook* approached Gussie again in 1931 with the idea of producing a monograph on Narcissus, an idea which appealed to him as he had a long experience of collecting and growing them right back to 1891. His Alpine Meadow with its mass planting of daffodils and the dwarf species daffodils, and the drive at Myddelton which he had planted himself by bowling the bulbs under-arm and planting then where they fell to make them look natural, are two of the spring glories of Myddelton. Any boys visiting him at this time were always allowed to take bunches of them home to their mothers, but only a few from each clump so as not to spoil their appearance.

To the question "what is the difference between a Narcissus and a Daffodil?" Gussie quoted the seventeenth-century apothecary John Parkinson: "many idle and ignorant gardeners ....doe call some of these Daffodils Narcisses, when as all know that know any Latine that Narcissus is the Latine name and Daffodil the English of one and the same thing". *The Handbook of Narcissus* was published in 1934. It had been ten years since the *Crocus Handbook* and both contained marvellous drawings by him; this was a particular achievement because by 1934 the sight in his good eye had deteriorated considerably. Percy Andrews, another Bowles Boy from the 1920s, remembers Gussie's glasses as having only one lens for the left eye, the right aperture being empty, and that he used to spin them on his index finger. By now he could only see by means of spectacles, with a watchmaker's glass attached to them and by then placing himself very close to the subject.

For the first issue of Forty Hill School Old Boys' Magazine, Gussie was invited — no doubt by Mr A. Butcher, MC, who was by then the Headmaster — to write the foreword.   Typically Gussie rose to the occasion for in the edition published in December 1932 he wrote: "I have been asked to write a foreword for this new magazine.   It seemed an easy task, so I accepted the honour of laying the magazine foundation stone with my pen.   Now I am wondering how to set about it, and what ingredients I ought to mix for my imaginary mortar.   Some forewords are written by those who are privileged to be the first readers of a new work, and can direct the attention of later readers to the good things they have discovered in the book.

"This pleasant and easy way is denied to me for I must write ahead of the pleasure, i.e. of reading, and though I am convinced that there will be much to praise, I feel rather like the Irishman who said he preferred to prophesy after the event.

"However, weather prophets who are good at their job (for some are weatherwise and some otherwise) can foretell coming changes because they have a sound knowledge of past records and local conditions.   Have I gained sufficient knowledge of Forty Hill boys, Old Boys and young boys, the hims ancient and modern of the Parish, to foretell fair weather, the absence of all dull skies, storms and breezes, to produce the glorious sunshine of a brilliant success for the Old Boys Association and its Magazine?   Yes.   I confidently declare that if all my school friends of the last fifty years will join us in this venture we can bring about the finest harvest season that can be.

"A refreshing breezy Christmas Greeting from those in icebound Canada, in the next column to warm greetings from Australia's harvest fields will balance each other so pleasantly that the result will be 'set fair'.

"There is much that is sensible and good, as well as brevity, in the American way of introducing strangers 'Mr X meet Mr Z'.   Then both X and Z will say 'Vurry pleased to meet you'.   My foreword then shall become an introduction after this pattern.   I say to every Forty Hill Boy 'MEET YOUR MAGAZINE'.

"So now you must all say ' Very pleased to meet you', and remain its friend forever.

E. A. BOWLES"

Above: *E.A.B. on the steps of the Museum with Jack Walpole in the 1920s.*

Below: *Stalwarts of Jesus Church, Forty Hill, collecting money at a Myddelton House garden open day in the 1930s — left to right: Jim Wilson (verger), Mr Martin, William Radford, Mr Hardwick and Mr Byford (in the choir for sixty years).*

Gussie celebrated his seventieth birthday on the 14th May 1935 and the parish united in wishing him many happy returns by inscribing the names, 431 of them in all, in a handsome velvet calf-bound album, and for his garden they gave him a stone Japanese lantern.   So that everyone, even the poorest, might contribute the subscriptions were purposely kept low — 'up to a shilling' being the rule.   Writing in the parish magazine, the Revd E.A. Koch spoke for everyone: "We past and present inhabitants of Forty Hill, whose names are attached, are glad to take the opportunity afforded by your birthday to assure you of our high esteem and deep affection. Forty Hill and all who live in it owe you so much that we cannot think of it without remembering you. That you may have good health and every blessing is the wish of us all"

Gussie responded in the following issue in June:

"My Dear Friends,

"By kind permission of the Vicar (Rev. E.A. Koch, M.A.) I am using our magazine to thank you all for the pleasant surprise you gave me on the eve of my birthday.

"The beautiful album of signatures of so many of my best friends, who in the charmingly expressed good wishes, will always be one of my most valued possessions.

"I thank you also for the accompanying generous present, and from my heart for the assurance of affection of so large a number of good neighbours whose friendship and kindness to me have always done much to make my life here a happy one.

"Yours most gratefully,
        E. Augustus Bowles"

He put the lantern by the bridge, where the two lead Ostriches stood sentry. Gussie had his photo taken with it and sent it as a Christmas card.

Gussie's adored sister-in-law, Dolly, died in November. She was 69 and had always kept a maternal eye on him. "Gussie, you need a new suit", she would tell him and ignoring his objections send down one of Henry's. Gussie never bothered much how he looked and was the despair of his butler Morley who did his best to keep his employer as presentable as possible. Charlie Smith saw him arrive back at Myddelton from the funeral of a friend and immediately 'set to' weeding on his hands and knees in his best suit. Whilst the comb was

Above: E.A.B. with some of the Bowles Boys outside the Summer-house in the Rose Garden — left to right: Ted Sills, Bill Washington, E.A.B., Leslie Everett and Sonny Harrington.

Right: E.A.B. with the granite Japanese lantern subscribed for by friends and neighbours to celebrate his seventieth birthday in May 1935. He used this photograph as a Christmas card.

anaethema to him, he would simply wet his hands and smooth his hair back to keep it in place. In his old age another quirk he acquired was the habit of cutting his own hair: feeling through it, he would enclose tufts of hair between middle and forefinger and snip it with scissors. Leslie Dale teased him once about his gloves through which his fingers protruded. "Well," he said, "I can't afford to buy new ones. I haven't got any money'.

Peter Deering recalls that in the study one evening after the war, Mr Coombs brought in a pair of grey flannel trousers. Gussie put his hand out to feel the material: "Oh yes, they feel fine, how much were they?" Mr Coombs said "twenty-two shillings, Sir," and Gussie nearly blew his fuse since he could not bear to think of spending so much money on a pair of trousers. It is probable that, although he was to leave assets amounting to £89,139 his fortune was tied up with the house and its contents and that he was only a rich man on paper.

Dolly was laid to rest in the vault to the right of Jesus Church. The unfortunate level of the water table on that day caused Gussie to remark that he would not make this his final resting place.

Meanwhile Bob Sills, the boy whom Bowles all but adopted, had been pursuing a career in the RAF. He had studied hard at Ponders End Technical School and went on to pass his entrance examinations and went on to Halton. By 1936 he was Leading Aircraftman Sills and stationed at R.A.F. Martlesham. He had also been wooing a charming girl called Audrey Roberts, who had agreed to marry him. Bob asked Uncle G to be his best man — "You want someone younger," came the reply — "You're young enough" — Gussie was delighted. For a wedding present Gussie gave them return tickets to Cornwall where they honeymooned in a smuggler's cottage in Portreath, from where the happy couple sent a postcard to Gussie. "Audrey and I wish to thank you again for everything and especially for yesterday for I forgot to toast the Best Man and the finest and best gentleman and friend one could ever have. The very best to Uncle 'G'. Audrey and Bob."

Morley, Gussie's faithful butler, died on 20th February 1938. He had come to Myddelton from brother Henry's town house and had served the Bowles family for forty years having replaced 'Old Davis' before him. Gussie invited his former footman, Ernest Coombs, to fill the gap in his staff. He was working at the Royal Small Arms Factory at the time but left immediately to resume work for Gussie.

9

Hitler's War

The coming of the Second World War and conscription saw the domestic staff diminished by one but otherwise things remained as usual: Swatton, Sam Howard and Jack Whitbread, who had been under-coachman and was made a gardener after the death of H.C.B. Bowles, and Fred Redmore, who was transferred from the garden to become chauffeur and was living in the Gate Lodge until he was called up.   John Rogers, himself a Bowles Boy, was also on the garden staff.   As Miss Dean was not well, Florence Darrington was promoted to cook (her wages of 7s.6d per week in 1925 having risen to £1 in 1945).

During the war, Gussie found listening to the wireless "a great joy. I find I can't write and listen too, so I listen and rest my eye." The black-out didn't help: "I'm more blind and in these dark days things take much longer to do." He was now wearing spectacles fitted with a steel plate with a pin hole, to concentrate the remaining sight of his good eye.

A sudden and serious illness struck him in the middle of an air raid on 3rd September 1940, a year to the day after war was declared. Gussie was sheltering with Fred Redmore and his wife in the basement of Myddelton when he was suddenly seized with agony, but he wouldn't let Fred out to call for a doctor until the all clear had sounded.   A double hernia was diagnosed.   All local hospitals were full and the only place a bed could be found was Onslow House, Southgate — a maternity hospital.   One friend could not resist asking him "Well, how is the baby?"

Florence Darrington remembers how the privations of the war affected life at Myddelton: "We didn't have any more than anybody else because, I mean, the butcher only let us have our rations but, of course, having the farmyard, we used to have the chickens.   But we weren't allowed to kill the pigs and if we did we had to give some of it up: we weren't allowed to keep the whole pig.   But we used to make do.   We had the dairy you see, we had eggs so we could make lots of dishes, soufflés and things and we always had vegetables for making soups and nourishing bits and pieces.   Mr Gussie's favourite part of the chicken was the liver.   Sometimes I didn't serve them if I thought they weren't good and he would say: 'I don't suppose this chicken had any liver!' With the war on tradesman did not deliver, except the baker. I cycled to the butcher for the meat ration, Waltham Cross for the fish ration and Forty Hill for the ration of groceries which took up a lot of my time each week."

Gussie then revived the project for the Anemone book from sixteen years before. He had brought back dried specimens of them from his plant-hunting travels and pressed and stored them in large envelopes accompanied by his detailed notes and observations. Frances Perry, who was living at Bulls Cross cottage since she married Gerald, was now coming to Myddelton to be 'his eyes', for he now had to lean his head on the page to write. Frances busied herself typing up his notes as he completed them. As his eyesight faded, so his other senses sharpened and he learned to identify plants by smell and tasting the leaves.

A regular guest at Myddelton was an old friend Arthur Robinson from his Cambridge insect-hunting days. He arrived in February 1942 when his house was requisitioned and he stayed until he could find another. He was still there in 1944. "He used to have a box of whisky," recalls Charlie Smith, "and ask Coombs to smuggle it into the house". Gussie was teetotal. "Gussie used to ask Coombs to tell Mr Robinson not to lean back on his chairs since it weakened them." Robinson had done it once and the antique chair had disintegrated, dumping him on the floor.

Not only Robinson's house had been requisitioned. The Ministry of Works and Building was requisitioning gates and railings all over the country for the war effort. In January 1942 a letter arrived from the Ministry to the effect that the beautiful cast iron gates and railings bearing his father's monogram would have to be removed. Gussie appealed and a letter dated January 1942 from Enfield Urban District Council confirmed that "the gates and railings have been inspected by the architect who has decided that the railings on the dwarf wall should be removed, but that the gates shall remain". Perhaps the influence of his brother Henry, no longer an MP but still a Justice of the Peace, prevailed for the order was revoked. Ironically none of the metal confiscated was ever used for the war effort and many beautiful examples of the craft were lost needlessly.

Two or three days of Gussie's working week were still claimed by Wisley and the RHS committees and he was now vice chairman of the Chelsea Physic Garden Management Committee. It was still very much a full life.

Gussie in the garden of Myddelton House with his brother, Sir Henry, who was twice M.P. for Enfield. The only known photograph of them together after 1887, it appeared in the Enfield Gazette in June 1939.

On the 15th October 1943, Gussie's brother Henry died at the age of 84. He left the Forty Hill estate and the bulk of his wealth to his grandson, Derek Henry Parker Bowles. Henry's daughter, Wilma Mary Garnault, had married Eustace Parker, a solicitor by profession and grandson of the Earl of Macclesfield, on the 11th June 1913. Their first child was Derek Henry, and Daphne Wilma Kenyon was born 4th December 1917. With no male heir to carry on the family

*Derek and Ann Parker Bowles and their family in 1955
at their Newbury home, Dorrington Castle House.*

name, in 1920 Eustace Parker assumed the surname Bowles by royal licence. Derek married Ann de Trafford in February 1939, and their children were Andrew Henry born 1939 and Simon Humphrey born 1941, Mary Ann born 1946 and Richard Eustace born 1947. Following the death of his grandfather, Derek Parker Bowles moved to Forty Hall from Winterton Lodge where he and Ann had moved after their marriage. In Sir Henry's will, Gussie was left an annuity of £300 a year.

For the local and able-bodied of Bulls Cross, a rota was drawn up by Frances Perry for fire-watching duties. For the Myddelton staff, the beat was Bulls Cross to Maiden's Bridge. On these evenings Gussie posted himself on his front doorstep and would not go indoors until they were all safely back. "He took care of us, he really was like a father to us — always," recalled Florence Darrington. During the air raids she remembered "we had all those windows blown out in the morning room at one point and, at the back, that beautiful stained glass was blown out. Another time I was working at the kitchen table one day when they dropped a bomb at Theobalds Park, the blast seemed to take me from one end of the kitchen to the other. It was frightening." "Puffed in" was the way Gussie described the damage to his back windows after the V2 explosion on New Year's Eve 1944.

In the Middle East, Bob Sills had risen steadily through the ranks from pilot officer in 1941 to Acting Squadron Leader in 1944. As Officer Commanding 5 E.R.S. he had done much to promote Anglo-Egyptian unity, organising entertainments for off-duty hours as well as football and cricket matches. Where previously morale had been low, it now soared. Before being appointed Commanding Officer, he had investigated serious engine problems on Kittyhawk aircraft and the losses of Ventura aircraft on anti-submarine patrol in the eastern Mediterranean. After VE Day, he used his leave to visit Gussie and met him in the rock garden, where he found him characteristically bent over, face close to ground, grubbing out weeds. Bob whistled, automatically Gussie whistled back and turning his head, said "Who is it?" "Bob," was the reply. He rose and clasped Bob's outstretched hand. "Dear old lad'. Bob picked up Gussie's trug and they walked back to the house.

10

An "Octogeranium"

Shortly afterwards, Gussie celebrated his eightieth birthday. The church magazine recorded the event with: "All the inhabitants of Forty Hill will unite in congratulations and hearty good wishes to one who was born here and has lived all his life here, making friendships in ever increasing attachment'.

With the return in 1946 of William T. Stearn from the RAF in Burma, work resumed on the Anemone book.   Stearn stayed several weeks at Myddelton to help Gussie. They began work at 10 a.m. in the morning room and a long trestle table was spread with their material. On it clearly displayed was a notice for Alice 'please do not touch'. They would work until 11 at night, with occasional strolls in the garden to find live material. Remembering their close working relationship 46 years later, Professor Stearn wrote: "I took down from Bowles everything that Bowles could possibly dictate relating to Anemones.   Then I was recalled to the Royal Horticultural Society, and there was never time allowed to get it completed. If I had stayed at Myddelton another three months, then the whole book would have been completed. It never was, and I am rather sorry about it, because it would have been a nice book and a fitting memorial to Bowles."   Yet their work did bear fruit in two papers for the *RHS Journal* on "The history of *Anemone japonica*" and "*Anemone hortensis* and *Anemone pavonina*: a history of confusion'.

Following the disappointment of the Anemone book, Gussie learned that Frederick Stern was planning a study of the genus Galanthus (Snowdrop). Gussie's gardening lists record that he was growing them from 1892 and many recognized him to be an authority on the subject. Writing about them in *The Garden* in 1907, he could boast "my garden has never been without snowdrops since the end of October, and now, on April 16th I still have a few blooms of *G. ikariae* in good condition". His method of increasing them, he would tell beginners, was simple: "stir them up!" A collaboration was suggested by Stern and happily Gussie accepted. The only things troubling him were his age and eyesight. Starting initially by correspondence, they then worked at Myddelton, sitting at a table with a shaded oil lamp between them, Stern's wife taking down their notes as the two ratified their findings. Perfectionist that Gussie was, he preferred to work with live specimens rather than consult the 'mummies' preserved on herbarium sheets. Stern however was impatient to complete the book and increasingly took over the project — stifling Gussie's enchanting

*The author with Professor William T. Stearn in the Alpine
Meadow at Myddelton House in 1985.*

descriptions based on his personal observations of many years living on
intimate terms with his snowdrops. When the book was published two years
after Gussie's death, of the 28 colour illustrations Gussie had selected only two
were published. As Gussie had feared, his piece on "Garden Varieties of
Galanthus" with names and references, which appeared as Chapter VII in F.C.
Stern's *Snowdrops and Snowflakes*, turned out to be "dry and confusing". For
the book's failure to achieve mass appeal we have to look in Stern's direction.

On his return from the forces Charlie Smith came to Myddelton as a full-
time gardener. He was also given the part-time job of chauffeur after the tragic
death of Fred Redmore, who was cycling to his mother's house in Bulls Cross
during a gale when a large branch from a beech growing in Frances Perry's
garden fell, crushing him to death. Typically Gussie immediately arranged a
pension for his widow Margaret that was to continue to her death. Fred had
once been given the afternoon off by Gussie to drive him to the Embassy
Cinema, Waltham Cross, to watch *Snow White and the Seven Dwarfs*. It was
the only film Gussie ever saw. "He was very proud of that!" Charlie told me.

E.A.B. and his crocus frame — a photograph taken by Peter Deering in 1950.

Perhaps not surprisingly, as a consequence of the many committees Gussie sat on with their attendant excursions to the RHS Halls in Westminster, to say nothing of his constant battle to keep the weeds down in his own personal preserve, the rock garden, Gussie became confined to bed with a strained heart. The discovery, made during his 'monthly overhaul' by his doctor at Easter 1951, forced him into reluctant rest.   A bed was brought down and placed in the morning room and, after a fortnight, he was permitted to sit up for luncheon, tea and supper and to lie on the couch occasionally.   In the *Daffodil Year Book* of that year, he wrote: "when the sun shines, it is very pleasant through the bow window".   And further on ... "I missed not only the out-of-doors joys of April and May but also the RHS show".   Not least he was to miss the Chelsea Flower Show for the first time in his long working association with the Society.

On 21st October he wrote to his great-great-nephew, Andrew:

"My Dear Andrew many thanks for your letter. I am glad to know that you are getting your garden in order after its long holidays. I send you a bulb or two for it, and hope they will please you when they flower.

"Your Dad looked in and had tea with me on Thursday on his way to

Brigadier Andrew Parker Bowles at Myddelton House in October 1995 with the author, Christine Barker (the Head Gardener) and Simon Parker Bowles.

London from Newmarket and I thought he was very well.

"I have had a bad boil on my foot and can't get a shoe on it and have to hop about on one shod foot and the bad'un in a slipper - so I can't do very much good garden work. I have some good flowers of *Nerine bowdenii* out now & crocuses of several kinds and the autumn snowdrops, *Galanthus olgae* are good this year. The weeds are the largest I have ever seen. Groundsels like trees and tigers could hide under the Gunnera leaves. Good luck to you and the garden.

Yours loving old uncle A.B."

He was hoping against hope that Andrew would continue the love and fascination for gardening that had propelled him all his life; sadly it has not had the same deep allure for him.

Andrew Parker Bowles recalls the joys of visits to Myddelton House when he and his parents were living at Forty Hall after the death of Sir Henry Bowles in 1943. E.A. Bowles, as always, knew how to interest and amuse young boys.

"My brother and I would walk down and look for him. We would find him, trail along behind him, and then go into the house; he always had sweets and things which he used to give us. I remember he gave me a birds' egg collection and my brother a collection of shells. Every drawer was packed with marvellous things — a bronze, birds' skeletons, and everything a little boy loved. When I was away at school he used to send me bulbs and plants in funny old parcels, with things falling out of them. Not surprisingly, I used to win the school gardening competition — it was about the only thing I did win — with E.A. Bowles's plants against everybody else's cornflowers and lettuces.

" I remember asking, as small boys do, what was the rarest plant he had. I think he said it was a double orange celandine, and he took me down to the rockery to see this very ordinary-looking flower. I learned a lot about gardening just by trailing along behind him, and gardening was my favourite occupation at school. I think I then knew a lot more about practical things like taking cuttings than I know now. I looked forward to those regular Myddelton visits. I learned a lot about plants, particularly crocuses and daffodils, the breeding of them and crossing them and all that sort of thing. It was a very interesting time, and of course it is now nearly fifty years ago. When I was at Ampleforth, I got very involved in helping to make a garden out of a hillside, which is still there; but I don't think I have the imagination or ability to be a garden designer. I've always been interested in plants, though."

Revisiting the place in 1995, Brigadier Parker Bowles spoke of his memories of Myddelton House:

"The house itself was quiet, with a very nice smell, but always dark. We used to come in here to the front room, looking down towards the small lake, or into his study where he used to have drawers full of every sort of thing, including chocolate. In the billiard room in the stable-yard, there were stuffed animals and birds.

"My great regret is that I didn't appreciate who he was and what he had achieved in the field of horticulture. I just thought of him as my great-uncle, that was all; one didn't appreciate that he was a world-famous figure, you know. Gardeners in countries around the world prick up their ears when I say I'm related to E.A. Bowles. Its rather flattering."

Gussie spent Christmas of 1951 at Forty Hall, with Derek and Ann Parker Bowles and his great-great nephews. A shadow hung over the celebrations: it was the knowledge that he would not see Derek and Ann for some months as Derek was to receive treatment in Switzerland for pulmonary tuberculosis.

E.A.B. standing by the New River in the 1950s.   He is holding his own invention, a two-pronged hand-fork.

The following years were to be punctuated with many such stays in hospitals and sanatoria.

In May 1952 Bob Sills came to say good-bye before being posted to Singapore. A Squadron Leader, OBE now and twice Mentioned in Dispatches, he was told by Gussie: "you'll be an Air Commodore yet!" Gussie walked down with Bob to 'Swatton's Gate' — the name stuck although Swatton had retired three years before and John Rogers was now head gardener. When they reached the gate, Gussie grasped Bob's hand with both of his and said: "We'll meet again.......across the wide river". His last words to Bob were "good-bye, dear old Bob". Bob left him and cried on the way home. "I don't suppose I shall ever see him again," Gussie told John Rogers. In that month of May 1952, Myddelton was being advertised under the National Garden Scheme: "May Sat. 10th Myddelton House, Bulls Cross, Enfield 2-7 p.m. Rare Plants and Trees. Personally conducted tour of Garden by Mr Bowles at 3 o'clock 6d extra. Liverpool Street to Enfield Town then bus 310. Stop: Turkey Street. Green Line 715 Stop Turkey Street."

Peter Deering remembers those garden open days when as a boy he would help out: "I would be given the job of collecting the tickets from people who paid for a conducted tour by Gussie round the gardens and then following on in the wake of the group to ensure that they kept together and that strays did not join without paying their sixpence. Gussie would do two, perhaps three, tours each afternoon. At the appointed time quite precisely, he would emerge from his study (or we would all emerge from his study) and pick up a silver bowl which stood on the table in the hall, and Gus would go out onto the front steps, hands behind his back which was his favourite stance, and welcome everybody and give them a very short introduction. And off we'd set and, of course, he knew to the inch where every plant was and what state it would be in at that particular time. It really was quite a remarkable feat."

Visitors were still welcome. Lord Morton came in July — the two had met four years before on the joint Iris Committee on which they both served. Morton visited the garden two years later having been told to 'bring a basket' to take away sundry bits and pieces. "Is it big enough?" Bowles would ask. For all his knowledge, Morton recalled, he never laid down the law and was always ready to listen to young ideas. On this visit Morton remembered remarking on the pink flower of a greater bindweed flourishing on the rock garden — it shouldn't have been there but it looked so beautiful. "Yes", said Bowles, "I come out here sometimes and do an hour's weeding and when I finish I think I've spoilt it all". Once when a visitor told him how much he admired a plant at Myddelton but could not grow himself, Gussie was blunt in his prognosis: "you keep your garden too tidy!"

11

The Final Years

For some time Gussie had been worrying what would become of his garden after his death.   Some hope had materialised with Abercrombie's *Greater London Plan* of 1944 according to which the Bowles estate would be preserved in the Metropolitan Green Belt, but that was all very much up in the air.   As luck would have it, Professor Jim Fairbairn of the University of London's School of Pharmacy called at Myddelton in January 1950 in search of Chinese Rhubarb, having been advised to try Gussie by Bill MacKenzie of the Chelsea Physic Garden who knew he had much better specimens. The two men got on very well and Fairbairn paid several visits, on one occasion asking Gussie what would happen to the garden when he was gone.   Gussie unburdened himself and Fairbairn suggested that the University, which was at that time looking for a site within easy reach of London to grow medicinal plants, might be interested in purchasing the house, garden and adjacent fields. It was the answer to Gussie's prayers, but dare he hope? Negotiations began between the Royal Free Hospital Medical School and the School of Pharmacy together with Gussie and his solicitors.   It was slow going but by February 1953 agreement was reached by all sides whereby the house and grounds would transfer on his death to the University of London. More important than anything else to Gussie was the promise that his great living masterpiece, the garden, would be perpetuated. The relief renewed him.   Charlie Smith drove him to his RHS meetings and to Chelsea Physic Garden where he enjoyed going round accompanied by MacKenzie, and spending more time with his newly retired 'artist friend', Gerard Parker.

However by October 1953 he was writing to Derek Parker Bowles in an almost illegible hand: "I hope Ann was not much shocked by me having gone so far downhill and to be now such a feeble chronic invalid. So far — except that I lose the word I want for some minutes — my headpiece is still working, but I shuffle along bent nearly double to see where I put my feet, can't use my left arm to throw things and to get in and out of clothes."

That Christmas he had lunch with Gerald and Frances Perry at Bulls Cross Cottage, leaving at 4 o'clock "as the fire would be ready in his study". He was, as he described himself in a letter to Dick Trotter, "a poor old cripple who scuffles along, has balancer trouble of the ears, very blind and a bit deaf, and I fear very irritable, but clinging to life with great obstinacy".

In a letter to his great-great nephew, Andrew, dated 16th January 1954, he wrote:

"Dear Boy,
"Here are the daff. bulbs I put aside for you — a bit late but the big chaps will flower I hope and the small fry should grow on and do well next year. Nimrod is one of the best and largest of the Lanarth seedlings.
      Anyway good luck,
        Your loving uncle Gus."

The following month his devoted butler Coombs died. He had tried to keep his heart trouble from Gussie until the day it became evident that the heavy silver tray and the staircase were too much for him. Typically Gussie insisted a couch be put in the servants' hall for him to rest on. Coombs's style of butlering was in marked contrast to William Morley who was inclined to be stately and dignified. He is remembered still for his legendary wafer-thin bread and butter and Gussie adored the inch-and-a-half square buttered slices, which were sometimes daintily rolled — Gussie preferred the squares which he always ate upside down "because that way you taste the butter better". Coombs's death was a sad blow. Gussie was ailing and shortly afterwards his legs failed him and visits to the garden necessitated a wheelchair.

Later that month he attended the RHS Annual General Meeting to present the Victoria Medal of Honour to the President, the Hon. David Bowes-Lyon, brother of the Queen Mother: "I feel very unworthy to present this, our highest honour, to one so eminent and so kind as he has always been. Perhaps I might be likened to the skull of the Mummy at the feast which the ancients had placed beside their good food to remind them they were getting on in years. I need no such reminder. You have only to look at me. I am almost ashamed to come and hobble about among you as I do, and if it were not for the kindness of all that I meet here at the R..H.S., who are always ready to give me a hand and keep my feet from stumbling, I do not know that I should be able to carry on. But if I give up the RHS and the pleasure I get from it, what will become of me? I do not think it would be worth living. Now that I know we have such an able President to look after our affairs, it does not matter if I get even a little older and am no longer able to come here." Few can fail to have been touched by the speech, for all could sense that the end was very near.

His final appearance at Vincent Square was on 13th April to chair the Library Committee and Scientific Committee. On 27th April it was reported to the RHS Council he had had a heart attack. William Stearn visited him on

2nd May and found him in bed in the morning room. He was tired but quite lucid, and at intervals spoke of different things — the merits of *Prunus avium* as a suitable rootstock for *Prunus sargentii*, of the Bowles and Garnault families, of his great-great nephew Andrew and his interest in natural history, hoping that Andrew would carry on something of him after he was gone, and his hope that Stearn would complete the Anemone book they had started.

Alice Mears, who nursed E.A.B. during his last illness.

Alice Mears was looking after him during the day and a night nurse was employed to ensure Alice got a night's sleep.   Florence Darrington never stopped visiting Gussie and remembered his last few days: "Alice said to me he's very ill. The doctor used to come in. But as he got towards the end he didn't want anything to eat. So on the Tuesday I went to see him. He fell out of bed so I helped Alice get him back: he was a dead weight. He said to Alice 'who's helping you?' She said 'it's Florence' 'Ah, dear old Florence' he said'."

On the morning of 7th May, with Charlie Smith at his side, he slipped into unconsciousness and died. It was a week before his 89th birthday. He loved May and once wrote "May is the supreme moment of the garden, just the climate one would expect to find in heaven".

In a letter to Bob Sills, dated 31st May 1954, the Revd W.B. Davies, Vicar of Jesus Church, Forty Hill, described Gussie's last hours:
"I always took the Blessed Sacrament to him each Sunday when he could not get to church. He asked me to be with him on the following day, when a specialist was seeing him with his own doctor and on the Monday I had a talk with the three doctors who said that although he was not responding to treatment as well as expected there was no cause for alarm and he might be back

to his garden again, but not walking. I was leaving that afternoon for three days at St Leonard's and when I bade him good-bye he was quite cheerful, frail of body but alert of mind. When I returned on the Thursday evening there was a note from my curate to say Mr Bowles was sinking. I went at once and could see that he was near the end, the change having come suddenly.

"He died at 11.40 a.m. Friday without regaining consciousness. He had led a good and useful life and many can thank God for the friendship of a real English Gentleman."

On the night before his funeral, relays of volunteers took it in turn to stand vigil by his coffin in Jesus Church. Frances Perry was among them. Despite the request for no flowers, a sheaf of them was placed on his coffin from Wisley, his second favourite garden. He was cremated on 11th May at Enfield Crematorium and his ashes placed in the rock garden at Myddelton, under the shade of a quince tree.

In tribute to him, Gussie's old friend David Bowes-Lyon wrote:

"His knowledge of garden plants was wide and deep and both scientific and practical. Throughout his long life he had lived at Myddelton House and had grown there most plants of any merit which will survive out of doors in the Home Counties. About each plant he knew not only practically everything which is to be found in literature, but also those things which are learned only by those who garden with their own hands. He could, and did, talk about plants in a most entertaining manner, and it was virtually impossible for anyone, however knowledgeable, to spend many minutes with Bowles in his garden without being impressed by the vastness of his knowledge, and without acquiring some interesting and worthwhile information. As might be expected, his garden was full of choice and uncommon plants, and nothing gave Bowles greater pleasure than to share them with others who would appreciate their worth. He was accustomed to greet a visitor with: 'I hope you've brought a basket' for he did not like any fellow gardener to go away empty-handed. Then, with his visitor, he would set out on a tour of the garden, armed with an old digging fork which had been cut down to two tines to adapt it for lifting pieces of plants without causing undue disturbance."

The RHS deliberated for some time on how to commemorate Gussie, finally deciding to create a living tribute to him in a corner of the garden at Wisley. They filled it with the 'demented plants' Gussie had collected over the years. From Myddelton House were brought those plants named by him

*One of the last photographs of E.A.B.,
taken in March 1954.*

and after him, like his black-faced pansy, *Viola* 'Bowles Black', the wall-flower *Cheiranthus* 'Bowles Mauve' (which he never grew), and the twisted hazel, under-planted with his favour-ite crocuses and cyclamen. This quaint and celebrated garden was completed in Sep-tember 1957 and named 'Bowles' Corner'.

After Gussie's death, the contents of the house were auctioned by Bowyer and Bowyer on three consecutive days in September 1954 and con-sisted of 920 lots. As was the family custom, all the servants were pro-vided for in his Will drawn up in the year be-fore his death:

Francis William Wallis (the cowman) £52 per annum
Margaret Redmore £39 per annum
Sam Howard £150 per annum
Ernest John Coombs (the butler) £150 per annum
John Rogers £150 per annum
Alice Mears £150 per annum
Charles James Smith £150 per annum
Daphne Wilma Kenyon Poole £100
Sqn Ldr Robert John Sills £100
Miss Florence Darrington £50

"To the vicar and churchwardens of Jesus Church towards the restoration Fund £50"

Alfred Swatton £52 per annum

"To the Royal Horticultural Society all drawings, manuscripts and printed documents relating to Galanthus"

"To W.T. Stearn, at present employed at the British Museum, all my drawings, manuscripts, printed documents, scrapbooks and collection of illustrations relating to Anemone to enable him to finish the book on Anemone."

In a codicil drawn up on 27th April 1954 his cook Hermione Wiltscho was given a £100 legacy.   Alice Mears was left the furniture in her bedroom and two sets of bed furnishings (two sets of sheets, bolsters, pillow cases and blankets). Squadron Leader Bob Sills donated his legacy towards the purchase of a memorial screen to Mr Bowles at the rear of Jesus Church, depicting the Benedicite.   Thanks to the generosity of his principal heir, Derek Parker Bowles, many books and documents from Bowles's library were presented to the RHS Lindley Library and some to the Chelsea Physic Garden and the Department of Botany, British Museum (Natural History).   This was in accordance with intentions Bowles had expressed to Stearn but did not include in his will.   Lacking means to finish the Anemone book, Stearn passed the bequeathed material to the Lindley Library.

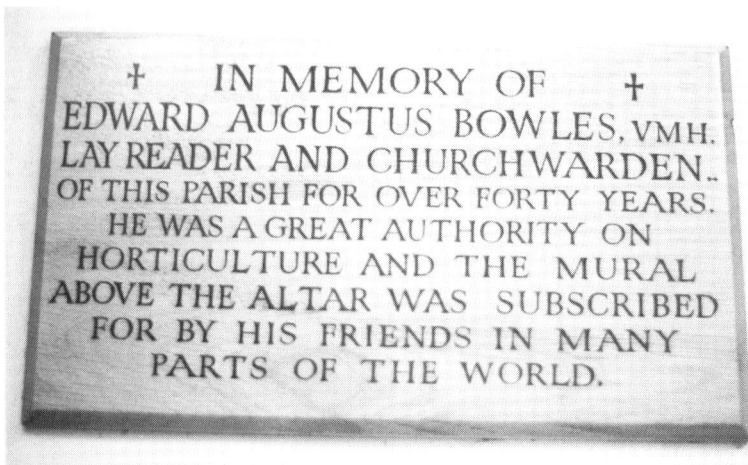

The memorial plaque in Forty Hill Church.

12

The Garden since 1954

The Royal Free Hospital School of Medicine and the School of Pharmacy jointly bought Myddelton House, the gardens and fields. What was the kitchen garden is now the Pharmacognosy Garden and is under the jurisdiction of the School of Pharmacy, funded by a grant from the University of London. Two joint committees were set up to administer the project — the Ground Committee from the School of Pharmacy and the Garden Committee from the Medical School, on which sat the Assistant Secretary of the respective school, *ex officio* the Deans and Secretaries of the schools and members of the academic staff. The independent chairman of the Garden Committee was William MacKenzie, then Director of the Chelsea Physic Garden. There was also a Garden Sub-committee which dealt with the day-to-day work of the main garden under the aegis of Frances Perry. This well-intentioned body ran the main garden from 1954 until its sale with the house to the Lee Valley Regional Park Authority in 1968. For a time the policy was that nothing should be touched and the hoe was a forbidden tool just as it had been in Mr Bowles time, but as Mrs Perry finally had to admit "you can keep the house as the master left it, but not the garden". In an effort to lessen maintenance, the box-edged beds on the New River terrace were ripped out as were the box hedges surrounding the Market Cross. Unfortunately there was neither sufficient funding to maintain the garden as Mr Bowles knew it, nor the justification for elaborate maintenance since the general public had limited access to the garden.

The Pharmacognosy Garden was administered at first by Mr Bowles's head gardener John Rogers, who had come to the garden as a schoolboy in 1915 and retired in 1966. Liberoso Guglielmi succeeded him until his return to Italy in 1970 and, since 1970, the garden has been administered by Charlie Smith, a Bowles boy and Gussie's one-time chauffeur/gardener, and an assistant. Since 1954 the fields at the back of the house have been developed into excellent sports fields for the Royal Free Hospital. The sports pavilion was built in the late 1960s — before then Myddelton House was used as changing rooms for the Sports and Athletic Club of the Royal Free Hospital and the Myddelton Cricket Club. Rooms at the top of the house also provided accommodation for a gardener and Mr Guglielmi and his family.

In 1859 the loop of the New River which ran through the grounds of

Myddelton House was bypassed by the construction of a long embankment across the Turkey Brook valley, downstream of the bridge at Forty Hill. This was part of a programme of works designed to shorten the course of the New River by avoiding the long detours up the valleys to the west of it. The abandoned channel through Myddelton was kept supplied with water at the cost of the Bowles family and, latterly, the Royal Free Hospital, and E.A. Bowles regarded it as an important feature of his garden. But by the late 1960s the Hospital no longer felt justified in paying this charge, and while the sale of the property to the Lee Valley Regional Park Authority was being negotiated this channel was filled in and laid to lawns. Fortunately the cast iron footbridge, dated 1832, still survives by the road boundary wall.

After the sale to the Lee Valley Regional Park Authority, the maintenance policies in the garden remained pretty much the same and one gardener, Eddie Piggot, ran the garden for fifteen years, his priorities being to keep the paths clean and cut the grass.

Starting in the 1960s, the garden was opened on one day a year for Snowdrop Day, an event organised by the Forty Hill Mutual Improvement and Horticultural Society. This continued till 1982 when the Regional Park Authority contacted Mr Christopher Brickell at Wisley with a view to getting advice on what should be done to restore the garden. A meeting was held in January 1983 and this was followed by a visit from committee members of the National Council for the Conservation of Plants and Gardens (London Group). The overall view of the garden gained from that visit was not all optimism. Many features had disappeared, most of the unusual plants for which the garden was famed had been lost or 'saved' by people not wishing to see them lost. More visits were made by the committee of the NCCPG and gradually their recommendations were acted on. In November 1983 the committee suggested the appointment of a Head Gardener who would liaise with and advise the Lee Valley Regional Park Authority and organise the restoration of the garden "in the style of Bowles."

On 1st April 1984 Geoff Stebbings, Kew Dip. (Hons), was appointed Head Gardener and with a staff of two gardeners. They began systematically to clear the beds of weeds, starting with the Rose Garden which led to the restoration of the pergola. Also in that year, a Garden Advisory Group was set up comprising representatives from the Enfield Preservation Society, the Forty Hill Mutual Improvement Horticultural Society, the National Council for the Conservation of Plants and Gardens, together with the Lee Valley Regional Park Authority staff, who were to contribute significantly to the development of the garden.

The garden staff at Myddelton House in 1954 — left to right: John Rogers, Sam Howard, Charlie Smith and George Tant.

Initial restoration efforts focused on the Rose and Pergola Garden, replacing roses that had come to the end of their life with species roses, renewing pergolas and re-laying the historic paving stones. A water supply was also established, with standpipes in several locations. With increased support from the voluntary societies, Open Days were increased to twelve per year and an initial leaflet on the garden prepared for visitors. Work continued apace and, in 1986, work began on the restoration of the pond, where dredging took place and a butyl lining was put in place.

By 1987 agreement was reached to open the garden on weekdays and a colour leaflet was prepared to publicise it. By this time, the Terrace Garden and the *Eremurus* and cactus bed in the Rock Garden had been restored, and an estimated 2,000 varieties of plants had been introduced into the garden. Most notable was the introduction of the National Collection of award-winning tall Bearded Iris, a project carried out in cooperation with the National Council for the Conservation of Plants and Gardens.   The Irises were established in the same beds where Gussie Bowles kept his. In addition, a plant record system was created, with each plant being given an accession number recording its origin and date of planting.

When in 1989 the Head Gardener resigned and following restructuring within the Horticultural Section, the garden became the responsibility of the Authority's Direct Services Organisation and was managed directly by the D.S.O. Manager.   However, in the autumn of 1993, the Direct Services Organisation was disbanded as a result of competitive tendering and the overall management of the garden became the responsibility of the Countryside Service of the Lee Valley Regional Park Authority. The two gardening staff continued to manage the garden on a day-to-day basis, with support from seasonal staff. At about this time, a conservatory from the Glasgow Festival was acquired and erected overlooking the pond, and pathworks were carried out.

In 1993, the 'E.A. Bowles of Myddelton House Society', a registered charity, was formed with the following objectives:

i)   to educate the general public by stimulating a greater interest and knowledge of the horticultural works and publications of the late Edward Augustus Bowles.
ii)   in furtherance of the above charitable object, but not otherwise, the Society may seek subscriptions and otherwise raise funds to establish a library and encourage re-publication of E.A. Bowles's horticultural books, promote lectures and displays relating to the life and horticultural works of E.A. Bowles as well as providing an educational and scientific facility, promotions of species of plants linked to the Bowles name, and facilitate public access to the garden created by E.A. Bowles at Myddelton House, Enfield, also to support and assist in the reconstruction, maintenance and development of the said garden for the benefit of the public at large, and to provide, or help to provide, equipment, plants and other features for the said garden at present in the ownership of the Lee Valley Regional Park Authority.
iii) doing all such other things as are necessary for the attainment of the above objects.

Unveiling the memorial seat at Myddelton House in the 1950s — standing (left to right): John Rogers (Head Gardener), Sam Howard, W. MacKenzie (Chelsea Physic Garden), and E. Etteridge (Forty Hill Mutual Improvement Horticultural Society); seated: Frances Perry, Dr Lloyd Williams and Professor Linnell.

    iv) to ensure, as far as possible, that the historic garden at Myddelton is maintained in perpetuity with access to the general public.

In 1995, the exterior of the Stable Block was restored, the courtyard refurbished and the clock brought into working order — part of the Stable Block now forms the office and rest-room for the garden staff.

The developing partnership between the E.A. Bowles of Myddelton House Society and the Park Authority in respect of the garden augurs well for the future development and restoration of the garden 'in the style of Bowles', both as a restoration and as a plantsman's garden.

Appendix 1

Key dates in the life of E.A. Bowles

1865   Edward Augustus Bowles born at Myddelton House, 14th May.

1873   Contracts an infection in his right eye — daily cauterisation results in partial blindness.

1881   Becomes a Sunday School teacher at Jesus Church, Forty Hill.

1882-84 Tutored for the Army and University examinations.

1884   Becomes an undergraduate at Jesus College, Cambridge.

1887   Graduates as Bachelor of Arts.
His brother John dies of tuberculosis at Myddelton House, 1 October. His sister Medora dies also of tuberculosis in Cannes, 27th December.

1888   Founds a Night School in Turkey Street for under-privileged boys and soon has ninety on the books.

1889   Joins his brother Henry and his wife, Dolly, on their honeymoon at La Mortola and goes on to Naples via Pisa and Rome.

1890   Starts to develop the garden at Myddelton House, beginning with the lower rock garden.

1893   Holidays with Henry and Dolly again to Biarritz, Bayonne and St. Sebastian, and his plant-hunting begins.

1894   Elected a Fellow of the Royal Entomological Society.

1897   Purchases Life Membership of the Royal Horticultural Society on 1st May.

1898   Plant-hunting with Dolly and Charles Gordon Shackle in Egypt, Malta, Greece, Italy and Switzerland.

1899   Elected a Fellow of the Royal Botanical Society of London.

1900   Elected to the RHS Scientific Committee in December.

1901   Starts the Plant Exchange Society, consisting of some 30 members who pass on a book in which they advertise their spare plants and requirements — its activities ceased in May 1907.
Elected a Fellow of the Royal Botanical Society.

1902   Elected a Fellow of the Linnaean Society.

1904   Elected to the Narcissus and Tulip Committee of the RHS

1907   Creates the pergola garden at Myddelton House.

1908   Elected to the RHS Council, 11th February; in the same year, also elected to the Floral Committee.
Begins to create the rock garden at Myddelton House.

1910	Plant-hunting in the Alps with Arthur Bartholomew and Hubert Edelsten; they are joined by Reginald Farrer. Founds the Forty Hill Mutual Improvement and Horticultural Society.
1911	Reginald Farrer dedicates his book, *Among the Hills*, to Bowles, referring to him as the "Crocus King." Plant-hunting on Mont Cenis with Arthur Bartholomew and Reginald and Sidney Farrer. Elected chairman of the RHS Narcissus and Tulip Committee. His mother dies, 4th October, aged 87.
1912	Bowles and Farrer go plant-hunting in the Tyrol and Cuneo. Invited by the editor of the *Gardener's Chronicle* to write about his garden in three (perhaps four) volumes.
1914	*My Garden in Spring* is published: Reginald Farrer's preface causes a furore. Plant-hunting in the Alps with the Garnett-Botfields.
1915	Appointed a Trustee of the Enfield Parochial Charities. *My Garden in Summer* and *My Garden in Autumn and Winter* are published.
1916	Receives the RHS Victoria Medal of Honour.
1918	His father, Henry C.B. Bowles, dies 1st February aged 87. Creates the Alpine Meadow at Myddelton House.
1919	Designs the Grenfell Medal for the RHS
1920	Reginald Farrer dies, aged 40, while plant-hunting in Burma.
1922	Plant-hunting in Lauteret with Richard Trotter, Susan Garnett-Botfield and Major Lawrence Johnston.
1923	Presented with the Veitch Memorial Gold Medal.
1924	*A Handbook of Crocus and Colchicum* is published. Plant-hunting at St. Remy in France with Susan Garnett-Botfield and Richard Trotter.
1925	Awarded a first-class certificate for *Crocus chrysanthus* 'Snow Bunting' and the Reginald Cory Cup for raising it. Curtis's Botanical magazine dedicated to E.A.B.
1926	Plant-hunting in Greece with Richard Trotter and his sister and Lady Beatrix Stanley. Elected a Vice-President of the RHS
1927	Plant-hunting in the French Pyrenees with the Garnett-Botfields, Lady Beatrix Stanley, Ned Rashleigh, F.J. Hanbury, Charles Lucas and Crump, his gardener.
1928	Awarded the Grenfell Medal struck in gold. Plant-hunting on the Italian Riviera, re-visiting La Mortola.
1929	Awarded the Grenfell Medal in bronze.

1930	Plant-hunting on the Italian Riviera, visiting La Mortola for the last time.
1931	Awarded the Grenfell Medal in bronze.
1932	Awarded the Grenfell Medal in silver.
1933	Elected chairman of the RHS Scientific Committee.
	Awarded the Grenfell Medal in silver-gilt.
1934	*A Handbook of Narcissus* is published.
	Awarded the Peter Barr Memorial Cup.
1935	His sister-in-law Dolly dies 1st November aged 69.
	Bowles celebrates his seventieth birthday: local friends and neighbours present him with a gold-tooled book of signatures and a granite Japanese lantern.
1938	Plant-hunting in Greece with Major Albert Pam — Bowles's last trip abroad.
1940	Accepts chairmanship of the RHS Library Committee.
	In hospital, 3 September, with a double hernia.
1943	His brother Henry dies, 15th October, aged 85.
1952	The revised edition of *The Handbook of Crocus and Colchicum* is published.
	Awarded the American Plant Life Society's William Herbert Medal for 1953.
1954	Attends his last two meetings at the RHS Halls, 13 April.
	Suffers a heart attack, 26th April.
	E.A. Bowles dies at Myddelton House, 7th May.
	Three hundred mourners attend his funeral on 11th May at Jesus Church, Forty Hill — his ashes are scattered on the rock garden at Myddelton House.

Appendix 2

Plants raised by E.A. Bowles or named after him

Anemone japonica 'Bowles White'
Anemone nemorosa 'Bowles Pink'
Buxus sempervirens 'Bowles Blue'
Carex stricta 'Bowles Golden'
Chrysanthus 'Blue Rock'
Chrysanthus 'Bumble Bee'
Chrysanthus 'Golden Plover'
Chrysanthus 'Khaki'
Chrysanthus 'Moonlight'
Chrysanthus 'Opal'
Chrysanthus 'Shot'
Colchicum 'E.A. Bowles'
Colchicum bowlesianum
Colchicum cilicicum 'Bowles Form'
Crocus 'Black-Backed Gull'
Crocus 'Kittiwake'
Crocus caspius 'Lilacinus'
Crocus chrysanthus 'Blue Jay'
Crocus chrysanthus 'Blue Throat'
Crocus chrysanthus 'Bullfinch'
Crocus chrysanthus 'Copenhagen China'
Crocus chrysanthus 'Eustace Parker Bowles'
Crocus chrysanthus 'E.A. Bowles'
Crocus chrysanthus 'Golden Pheasant'
Crocus chrysanthus 'John Hoog'
Crocus chrysanthus 'Siskin'
Crocus chrysanthus 'Snow Bunting'
Crocus chrysanthus 'White Egret'
Crocus chrysanthus 'Yellow Hammer'
Crocus korolkowii 'Dytiscus'
Crocus sieberi 'Bowles White'
Crocus tommasinianus 'Bobbo'
Crocus tommasinianus 'Versitom'
Cyclamen hederifolium 'Bowles Apollo Strain'
Daphne mezereum 'Bowles Variety'
Dianthus deltoides 'Bowles Form'

Erodium alpinum 'Bowles Form'
Erysimum linifolium 'Bowles Mauve'
Geranium 'Bowles' Variety'
Hebe 'Bowles' Hybrid'
Hebe 'E.A. Bowles'
Helleborus kochii 'Bowles Yellow'
Hemerocallis 'E.A. Bowles'
Iris germanica 'Ice Blue'
Iris germanica 'Myddelton Blue'
Iris reticulata 'Cantab'
Lavandula 'Bowles' Variety'
Lilium elegans 'E.A. Bowles'
Lilium x princeps 'Myddelton Form'
Malus 'Bowles Hybrid'
Mentha rotundifolia 'Bowles'
Milium effusum aureum, 'Bowles Golden Grass'
Narcissus 'Bowles Bounty'
Narcissus 'Bowles White'
Narcissus 'H.C. Bowles'
Oxalis 'Bowles White'
Papaver orientale 'E.A. Bowles'
Penstemon 'Myddelton Gem'
Philadelphus coronarius 'Variegatus' (Myddelton Form)
Phlomis fruticosa 'Edward Bowles'
Potentilla fruticosa 'Bowles Variety'
Primula x bowlesii   (discovered in the wild by Bowles and
                        Farrrer, who named it after Bowles)
Pulmonaria 'Bowles Blue'
Pulmonaria 'Bowles Red'
Pulmonaria 'Bowles White'
Ranunculus ficaria 'Bowles Double'
Rheum palmatum 'Bowles Crimson'
Salix 'Bowles Hybrid'
Santolina pinnata subsp. *neopolitana* 'Bowles Lemon'
Skimmia japonica 'Bowles Dwarf'
Tellima grandiflora 'Bowles Form'
Veratrum album 'Myddelton Form'
Vinca minor 'Bowles Variety'
Viola 'Bowles Black'
Viola 'Mrs. Bowles'

The above list represents the way Bowles's plants were known in his time.

Bibliography and Sources

Allan, Mea	*E.A. Bowles and his garden at Myddelton House 1865—1954* (London, Faber & Faber, 1973).
Aylott, Len	Letter from an Enfield weekly newspaper, c.1959.
Bowles, E.A.	Six pages of autobiography (MS in the Botany Library, Natural History Museum).
—.—	Crocuses (lecture in R.H.S. Journal, vol. 61, 1936).
—.—	*My Garden in Spring* (T.C. & E.C. Jack, 1914).
—.—	Unpublished correspondence with Sir Frank Crisp (MS in the Lindley Library of the R.H.S.).
Dale, Leslie	Notes of interview at Kirby le Soken, 1994.
Darrington, Florence	*Memories of Myddelton* (E.A. Bowles of Myddelton House Society, 1994).
—.—	Interview, 1 November 1994.
Forty Hill	*A Growing History: Memories of the Forty Hill Mutual Improvement Horticultural Society*, 1984.
Gough, J.W.	*Sir Hugh Myddelton: Entrepreneur and Engineer* (Oxford, Clarendon Press, 1964).
Illingworth, John and Routh, Jane	*Reginald Farrer: Dalesman Planthunter Gardener* (University of Lancaster, Centre for North-West Regional Studies Occasional Paper No. 19, 1991)
Leighton, Ernie	Interview, 9 October 1994.
Pankhurst, Alex	*Who Does Your Garden Grow?* (Earl's Eye, 1992)
Parker Bowles, Andrew	Interview with Brigadier Andrew Parker Bowles, O.B.E., 12 October 1995.
Perry, Frances	*E.A. Bowles and Myddelton House Garden* (R.H.S. Journal, vol. 79, 1954)
Quest-Ritson, Charles	*The English Garden Abroad* (Viking, 1992)
R.H.S. Journal	*E.A. Bowles 1865—1954, The Man and his Garden* (parts 1 & 2 in R.H.S. Journal, vol. 80, July & August 1955).
Rye, Joseph	*Recollections of E.A. Bowles* (MS written in 1975).
Slater, Reg	*Memories of Mr. E.A. Bowles and Forty Hill* (MS written in 1984).
Stearn, W.T.	*E.A. Bowles* (E.A. Bowles of Myddelton House Society, 29 February 1992).
Wagner, Henry	*Pedigree of Garnault* (Proceedings of the Huguenot Society of London, vol.XI, no.1, 1916)

Index